WORTH SHARING

WORTH SHARING

Essays & Tools to Help Project Managers & Their Teams

MIKE GREER

CONTENTS

DEDICATION

This book is **dedicated to all the project managers and project team members** who are struggling to make their projects less frustrating, more effective and less disruptive to their personal lives. I hope that somewhere in these pages are a couple of chunks of wisdom, some useful perspectives or some practical tools that will help you.

This book is also **dedicated to my kids and grandkids.** In these pages — especially in the "Peace of Mind" and the "Working with Your Team..." sections — I've compiled nearly everything I can think of that my life-scars have taught me about living or working effectively and peacefully. So, kids, if I've departed the planet by the time you finally decide to seek my advice, check out these pages. Most of what I'd tell you has been captured here.

— Mike Greer
July, 2015

INTRODUCTION

So... What's all this?

This is an idiosyncratic collection of blog posts, articles, essays, and handouts that I have created in the past two decades or so and shared through my websites. Some of these are excerpts from my books, some are stand-alone articles and some are handouts or tools that accompanied presentations I made in classes or at professional conferences and webinars.

Over the years I've received requests from webmasters, college professors, HR folks and in-house organizational trainers to link to some of these materials so they could share them with students, employees or visitors to their websites. Such requests I humbly granted, hoping that readers might find something valuable — something that would make their project work easier, their work with teams more effective or their interactions with difficult people a little less withering.

This book is an attempt to pull all this stuff together into a single document so that it is easily accessible to anyone, thus eliminating the need to search through my websites.

Caveat: You May Find Inconsistencies!

These documents were each written at a unique point in time and at a unique point in the evolution of my understanding. As the years passed I was inevitably confronted by unanticipated situations, feisty and contentious clients or students, grumpy fellow professionals, etc. These events and people challenged the assumptions I held and pushed me to rethink things. This change in my thinking, in turn, may have manifested itself in the form of inconsistencies from one of these documents to another, depending on when it was written. However, from my perspective, that's a good thing! Just ask Ralph Waldo Emerson, who tells us (my bold added):

*"A foolish consistency is the hobgoblin of little minds, adored by little statesmen and philosophers and divines. With consistency a great soul has simply nothing to do. He may as well concern himself with his shadow on the wall. **Speak what you think now in hard words, and to-morrow speak what to-morrow thinks in hard words again, though it contradict everything you said to-day...**"[from Emerson's classic essay, Self Reliance]*

In other words, it's okay to be certain and enthusiastic about a point of view and then change your mind about it later when new facts or new experiences come to light. And that's what I've done.

Anyway... Enjoy!

Despite the occasional inconsistencies among items, I hope you find something of value here. This collection represents my best approximation of wisdom and insight. In short, it's the stuff I believe to be **worth sharing**. Enjoy!

THE MEANING OF PROJECT MANAGEMENT

This Part of the book focuses on what Project Management (PM) means to me.

PROJECT MANAGEMENT: "A TECHNOLOGY OF MANIFESTATION..."

(Sometimes it takes someone on the outside looking in to provide you with that "whack on the side of the head" that changes the meaning of what you are doing. Such was the case with this simple email from a student.)

A while back I taught an online class based on my book, **The Project Management Minimalist**. After the class I received this email from one of the attendees:

"Thank you for your class, 'Become a Project Management Minimalist!' The practical tools and skills-in-attitude you teach are a source of inspiration and clarity for me. As a young project manager with a passion for social impact, I'm clear that the tools you share will help me become an effective presence for my community and teams. Project management as you teach it is truly a technology of manifestation! — Best Wishes, *Soheil Majd* "

As you might imagine, I'm always glad to get good feedback from a class participant. Most of the time, when I teach one of these online classes, I feel a bit like The Maytag Repairman: I'm fairly sure I provided a useful product, but I seldom hear much feedback from the attendees. But beyond the fact that someone took the trouble to thank me, Soheil's email really stuck with me. I found myself going back and reading it several times, largely because of the unusual perspective he expressed about the session.

Here are some of his unexpected insights that stuck with me:

> *"... practical tools and skills-in-attitude... are a source of inspiration and clarity..."*

Now I am well aware that my classes focus on practical tools and skills. That's no accident. I value the practical and the useful above all else. I've always believed that all the esoteric and complex PM theory is of absolutely no value if isn't embraced and easily put to use. So, the litmus test for me of any PM tool or practice is "Is this practical and useful in the real world?"

However, the phrase "skills-in-attitude" is a fascinating one! I am conscious that I try to share with my PM newbie students the attitude of "project manager as facilitator." And I'm also aware that I encourage PM newbies to apply all PM tools and processes gently and respectfully, so as not to get in the way of the smart people on their teams doing their jobs according to their professional best practices. But this phrase, "skills in attitude" was a wonderful leap that Soheil made — a real insight. The PM practice of an attitude of respect and deference toward the professional skills brought by the team, when applied repeatedly to each of the "nuts and bolts" tools I shared, turns out to be essentially a "meta skill." In other words, it's truly a "skill in attitude." Wow! Who knew?

"... *will help me become an effective presence for my community and teams.*"

Now translating this concept of "being a presence" in the real-world while inside a whirling, activity-filled project is difficult. The best a new project manager can do is simply be vigilant for opportunities to help... be alert to potential obstacles and remove them... be ready to fight for your team so they can do their work unencumbered by administrivia. I now see that all this translates to "become an effective presence for my community and teams." Well, said, Soheil!

"*Project management as you teach it is truly a technology of manifestation!*"

Now, to be honest, it is the sentence above that truly blew me away and caused me to re-read Soheil's email several times. As the years of my life accumulate and the miles traveled on the PM road pile up, I look back on all the folks I've tried to guide as they join me on this road. And what stands out above everything I've seen and done is that no matter how accurate we are in applying our official PM guidelines... no matter how religiously we apply our official PM best practices... we are in the business of manifestation!! New products, new processes, new events... all of these come into existence as projects. And to the extent that the soft technology (i.e., management practices) of PM support the birth of any of these new entities, they do indeed form a "technology of manifestation."

Reading Soheil's insights above, culminating in that incredible vision of PM as technology of manifestation, gave me a bit of a thrill! Think of it! If we practice this pursuit we call PM in an effective way, we manifest visions! Dreams of what might be are transformed into reality by our PM teams!

I've always been passionate about teaching my unique PM vision in my own peculiar way. And now thanks to Soheil's insights, I have been consciously connected to a formerly unseen, yet profound, theme that has been running through this vision all along! Wow! Who knew?

So the next time you're putting together a project charter or revising a project budget, take a moment and reflect on how you may be a bit like Leonardo. Think about how you might be manifesting a dream!

Thank you, Soheil!

Addendum: Cleaning Up Elephant Dung & The Thrill of Helping Smart People Make Beautiful Music

While PM at its most transcendent may indeed be seen as a "technology of manifestation," the PM practitioner should also be ready to grab a broom now and then and do the mundane work of keeping the team's path clear! (As you'll see below, this can have its own rewards.)

In my classes, as well as in the occasional interview, I love to make this analogy: A project manager should frequently behave like the guy in the parade who follows the elephants with a shovel, broom and wastebasket.

The project manager... following the elephants?

Picture this: A parade is in motion and features a marching band that will share their uplifting music with the crowd. Preceding the marching band is a beautifully-decorated group of elephants who, unfortunately, have no sense of propriety and release their waste somewhat at random. Now unless this voluminous elephant dung is quickly removed, the marching band may step in it and slip, fall, and ruin their performance.

It comes down to this: No matter how talented the band, they are going to need all the nasty elephant droppings removed from their path so they can keep marching and so their music can ring out and inspire the crowd. Without this humble street cleaner, all their musical talent and rehearsal could end in a discordant trip-and-fall disaster! It's a dirty job, but an important one — and someone's gotta do it!

So it is with project management. No matter how talented, how creative, how burn-the-midnight-oil your team is, if they are encumbered by obstacles, all their talent and creativity may never have a chance to shine. They need someone to "sweep the dung" out of their path! And when you, as project manager, are willing to jump in and grab a broom and start cleaning, you are likely to be rewarded with the thrill of seeing your team soar and dazzle with their work products.

The truth is I knew I was a true project manager when I realized that my sense of gratification and pride had shifted from doing great work myself to seeing great work created by a team whose path I had carefully tended.

My wish for you, project manager, is that you become comfortable with a broom and learn to thrill at your marching band's great music!

[Note: This essay was published as part of the #PMFlashBlog event "What does project management mean to me?" Learn more here: Free e-Book "What Project Management Means to Me" from #PMFlashBlog Authors]

THE PROJECT MANAGER AS PLATE-SPINNING JUGGLER

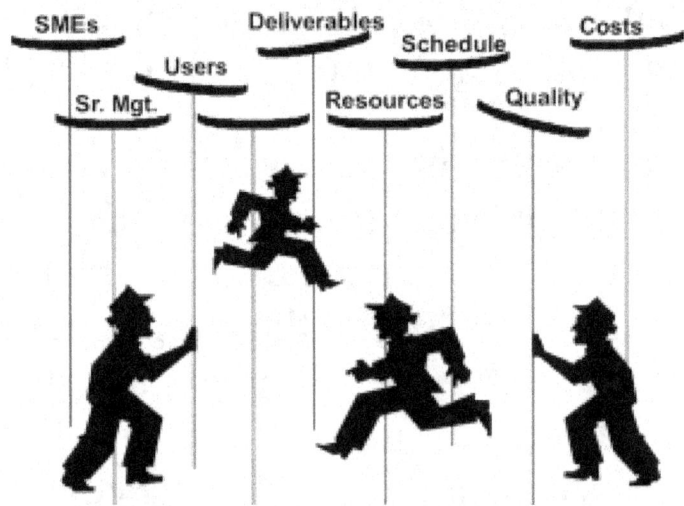

If you're a project manager then you know what it's like to feel frazzled, distracted and jerked in a thousand different directions. And you also know what it's like to watch other people doing the work of your project (creating the code, writing the scripts, building the prototypes, etc.) while you bounce back and forth among these folks looking for problems and figuring out how to remove obstacles. And you might be thinking that such a thankless existence is a bad thing that should be remedied.

But before you spend a lot of time searching for the latest "5-Step Plan for Controlling Chaos" let me suggest this alternative: Simply **relax into the blur that is your PM existence. Embrace it.** After all, it's completely normal... necessary... even desirable that someone with your judgment and experience play this part. This story from my first book, *ID Project Management*, explains:

"In the early '60s, when TV variety shows flourished, a strange little man would sometimes appear on Ed Sullivan's stage and fill it with plates rapidly spinning high atop long, slender poles. You may have seen him. He'd place a pole in a certain spot, then center a plate on top and get it spinning just so. Then he'd place another and another until the stage was filled with a forest of spinning plates on poles. He'd then scurry back and forth, finding plates that were slowing down and wiggling their poles until they began to spin rapidly again...

"Like the plate spinner, as project manager you are not directly involved in all actions while they are happening, but you do get each action started and you keep it going when it starts to slow down. And also like him, you must carefully plan all your moves. In broad terms, then, success as a project manager depends on these three activities:

- *Planning* — conceiving of the overall project and arranging for all project events to happen

- *Stimulating Action* — getting each individual event started at the scheduled time

- *Intervening* — observing when things aren't going according to plan, then taking action to get things back on track"

As this analogy illustrates, your consciousness as a project manager consists of continually stepping back and asking "What's next? What's slowing down or getting stuck? What should I do to keep things moving?"

When you contrast this with the role of an individual project resource, settled in, doing continuous uninterrupted work to create a new product or process, you can easily see why you life as the project manager could seem frazzled and disjunct. On the other hand, you get to orchestrate this stage full of spinning plates and observe the spectacle of them whirling in unison. How cool is that?

So the next time you are feeling frazzled and unappreciated you might want to think about the plate-spinning juggler. And while he himself didn't actually spin gloriously atop a tall stick, he did, for all his frenetic scrambling, create something amazing!

(Check out this YouTube video of a plate spinner, filmed at The Circus Space Cabaret, London.)

THE ORIGINS OF MY PM MINIMALISM: IT'S NOT MERELY SIMPLE-MINDED… IT'S ABOUT PM ESSENCES

The ability to simplify means to eliminate the unnecessary so that the necessary may speak." – Hans Hofmann

"Simplicity is the ultimate sophistication." – Leonardo DaVinci

"Everything should be made as simple as possible, but not simpler." – Albert Einstein

My Somewhat Jaded Perspective

As I grow older I am less inclined to seek anyone's approval for my professional opinions. I've got enough miles on my career to have come to my own conclusions about what matters most and to feel a certain confidence in these conclusions, validated by lots of experience. And I can distinguish valuable best practices from self-serving B.S.

One source of such B.S. is the tendency of consultants and professional certifying bodies, over time, to push and stretch their fields of expertise so as to cause them to become increasingly complex and impenetrable to newcomers.

Whether this drive for complexity is fueled by the experts' boredom and need for intellectual challenge or it is consciously contrived to create "client dependency" on the part of the newbies whom they are purposely baffling, it has the same result: It serves to ensnare anyone who steps into, and subsequently gets stuck in, the new conceptual webs.

Thus ensnared, the newbie-victims must purchase intricate tools and support services to unravel the mysterious new concepts, master them, and get "up to speed" on these latest and greatest methodologies. Having done so, the newbies are happy because they have acquired new tools and confidence. (Whether this confidence is justified or merely illusory is an open question!) At the same time, the consultants and professional organizations are happy, having taken on a new intellectual challenge, developed a shiny new conceptual system, and created a new business line and revenue stream. So it would seem that everyone wins when a field of practice such as project management (PM) becomes increasingly self-analytical and complex.

It's Minimalist... Not Simple-Minded!

On the other hand, I am haunted by those powerful quotes (above) from Einstein and DaVinci, et al that extol the virtues of simplicity. In fact, they imply that **the highest use of expertise and years of hard-won wisdom may be to reduce confusion... to "cut to the chase" ... to seek out the essences** that can best be discovered through the lens of sophistication and years of experience.

Now maybe it's my age and extensive career mileage. Or maybe it's my decades-long struggle to find ways to cut through PM complexity to help struggling newbies in my workshops become productive quickly. Whatever the reason, I find these quotes to be quite compelling. To me they are beacons shining a light toward a better way to approach PM. In short, those quotes embody the spirit in which my PM Minimalism was created.

Unfortunately, the word "minimalism" is easily misunderstood. Here's a frustrating example – a true story.

Recently I was sharing my career milestones with a respected senior-level management consultant whom I had just met. Before we spoke he had read my bio, investigated my work, and generally become familiar with my professional achievements.

Still, toward the end of our discussion, he admitted to having an "Aha" moment when he realized how the Project Management Minimalist concept had evolved. To paraphrase him, he said: "I'm honestly surprised at your depth of experience. To tell you the truth, 'Minimalist' could be taken to mean 'superficial' or 'overly simplistic.' So I wasn't sure how much you really knew about PM, since I only became acquainted with you through PM Minimalism. Yet after hearing about all your experiences in the PM field, I see how your Minimalist concept has evolved. And it seems well-grounded. It all makes sense."

"NUTS!" I said to myself after this discussion. Could other people be interpreting my use of the word "minimalist" to mean "superficial" or "simplistic?" For me, the word "minimalism" is all about finding the essence... the critical core... that which matters most! For me, PM Minimalism certainly is not superficial, but instead focuses on revealing PM essentials. And the formal definition offered by Wikipedia agrees:

"Minimalism describes movements... where the work is stripped down to its most fundamental features." (See http://en.wikipedia.org/wiki/Minimalism)

Exactly! That's what I'm talking about: PM stripped down to its most fundamental features. And there's nothing superficial or simplistic about it.

Who Am I to Reduce PM to Its Essences?

So what makes me think I'm qualified to strip PM down to its essences? That's easy. I'm older than many of the PM experts out there and I have seen waves of complexity come and go, then come back and go again! I've spent nearly three decades trying to help people apply PM in all sorts of fields and industries. What's more, I've got a long history analyzing and designing training and performance support systems in order to help people "cut through the crap" of all that "nice to know" stuff and find the "need to know… need to do" skills that enhance their productivity and effectiveness. (For a detailed audit trail, see "Addendum: My Long Journey Toward PM Minimalism" at the end of this book.)

The graphic below shows how my double career as both a "Skill Building Guy" and a "PM Guy" has meant that I've spent a long time creating results in both these domains. The Skill Building Guy has worked with subject matter experts in many different fields and industries to create the kinds of outcomes that professional training, HR and performance improvement people typically create. On the other hand, as I managed project teams to develop tangible, multi-media deliverables, I began to reflect on the PM process itself – to study it as a discipline and then to write about it.

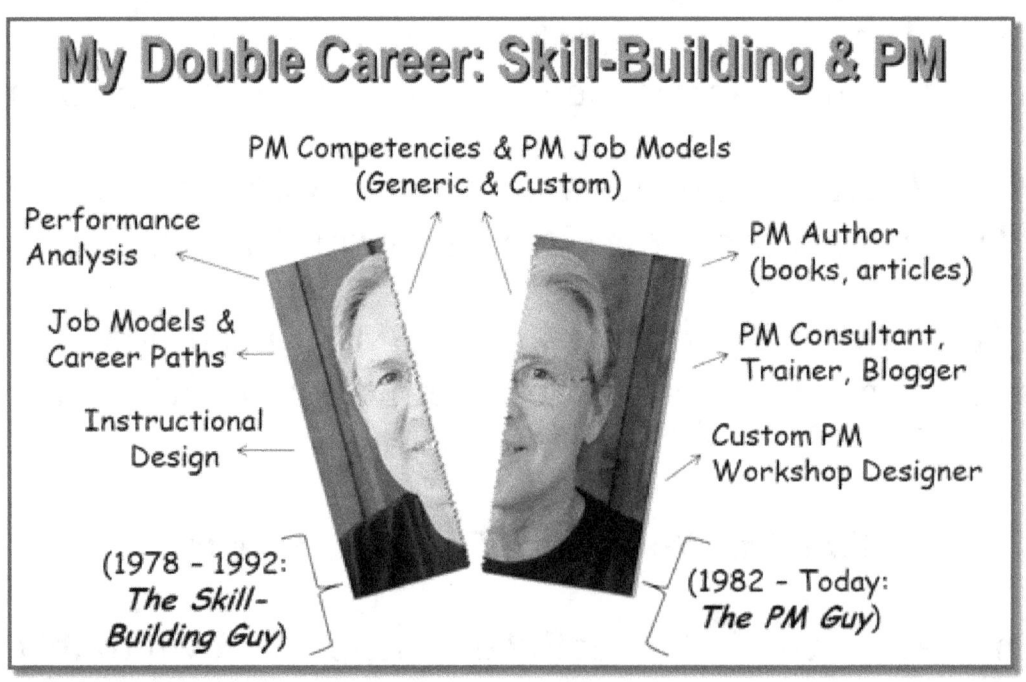

The result is that I've published many journal articles, countless blog posts, six books, lots of videos, dozens of podcasts and webinars – all in an ongoing quest to demystify PM and make it accessible to newbies.

Over the years, as a result of interactions with thousands of readers, media viewers, and training audiences, I've developed **two core values related to my work with PM:**

1. **Effective PM performance is more important than PM theory.** That is, what newbie project managers need is useful tools, not dense textbooks.
2. **I want to make sure PM stays out of the way of the expert practitioners.** Specifically, the skilled "worker bees" and SMEs who are working hard to create something new shouldn't be burdened by PM administrivia. At its best, PM should enhance, rather than smother, the work of project teams. At its worst, **PM for PM's sake is worthless!**

Seen through the lens of these values, **I have come to view all intentional PM complexity with skepticism.**

It Was My Students Who Taught Me to Simplify

Now, I haven't always felt this way. In the early days of my work as a PM consultant and trainer I was as impressed as the next guy with the complex, mysterious, and sometimes arcane practices advocated by the PM gurus and professional associations. After all, whose heart doesn't beat faster in the presence of an artfully-crafted earned value analysis or comparison of planned versus actual project progress? (*Really?*)

However, **as I spent time with classes of PM newbies** and helped them grow into more effective project managers, something magical began to happen. **All the superfluous complexity just naturally began falling away.** My students and clients, in their passion to do good and timely work in their areas of expertise, began pushing back against my official

PM process recommendations and insisted on dropping all the complex stuff that didn't work for them. They decided that these things just didn't matter.

So what was left? The most valuable essences of PM... the simplest, most powerful parts... the PM tools and practices that worked well, yet didn't get in the way.

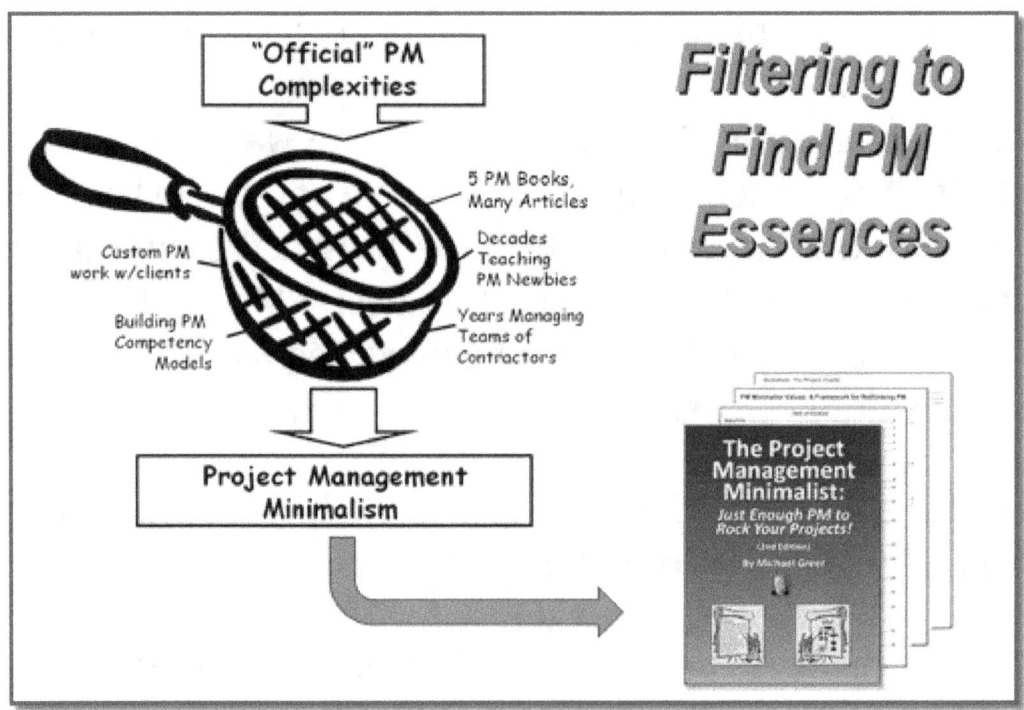

And **that's how PM Minimalism was born. I simply summarized and polished all the PM tools and practices that seem to have universal power for new project managers everywhere.** Then I ditched the rest! The following graphic illustrates the conscious and unconscious "filtering" processes that helped me shape my PM Minimalism.

What was left after this filtering process was similar to what is left when you convert a long-winded piece of prose into poetry: essences... clean, powerful, and yes, simple (though often profound) essences. What was left is the stuff that's fairly easy to do, stays out of the way, and enhances the work of the project team.

Now the good news is that you don't have to travel my decades-long path through the jungles of PM complexity to discover these essences for yourself. My clients, students, and colleagues have traveled that road with me and taught me all sorts of valuable PM lessons. Together we stumbled, fell, got beat up, and became scarred. And to honor our bruising journey, I have captured what we learned so you don't have to waste your time going down the same blind alleys we did.

The result? A tight little set of practices I call **PM Minimalism**. As I've said in the book, it's not rocket science! And (gasp!) it's so easy to apply you don't need consultants or trainers or (more importantly) costly and time-consuming PM certification to practice it.

But make no mistake. PM Minimalism is made up of the PM practices that are tried and true and universal. And practicing PM Minimalism will most likely get you some very good results with your project teams. And finally, while it certainly won't dazzle your local "born again" PMP who gets off on baffling his co-workers with esoteric PM terminology and arcane practices, PM Minimalism will gently guide your team and accomplish what the best management methodologies should always accomplish: It will help you get better results while remaining quietly unobtrusive.

As the graphic below illustrates, it's all about achieving "Just Enough" PM so that it does no harm.

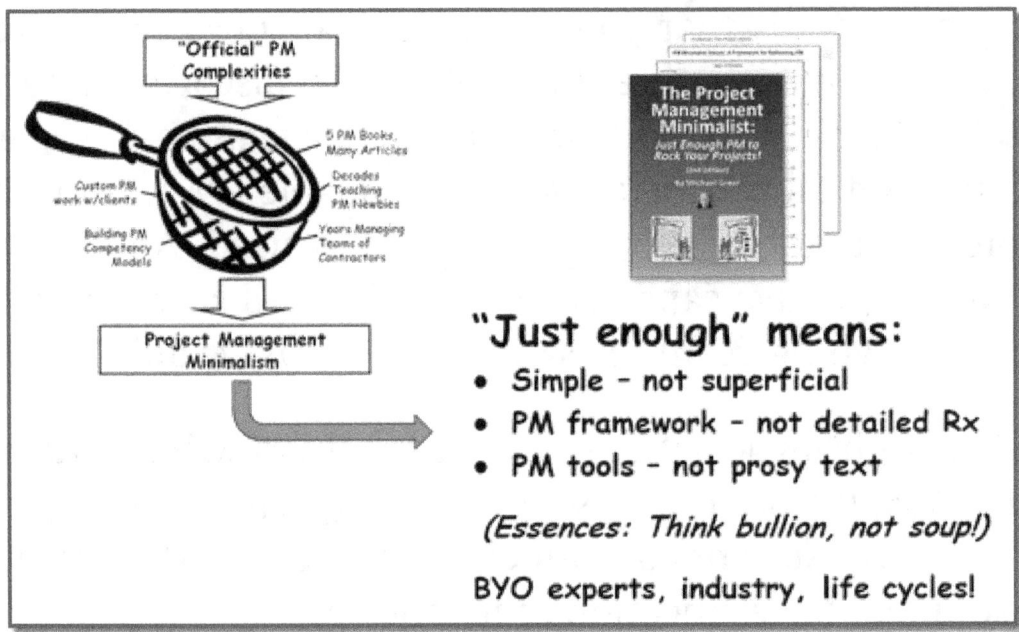

So now I say it loud: **I'm a PM Minimalist and I'm proud!** I'm proud to be getting the positive feedback from my readers and students, proud of the Minimalist's university book adoptions, and proud to be sharing these PM essences with overworked project managers and teams everywhere. If PM Minimalism helps to make their work lives a little easier and more productive, then all the effort's been worth it.

PM TECHNIQUES

This Part focuses on specific perspectives, strategies and tools that project managers or team members can use to better manage projects.

MY PM VISION & VALUES: 20 PRACTICES & ATTITUDES THAT MIGHT HELP YOU BECOME A BETTER PROJECT MANAGER

Here are some bits of Project Management (PM) wisdom I've accumulated over the years. I can trace each of them to a PM trauma, scar, hard-won victory, or a behavior pattern that seemed to consistently produce good results. I hope you find these valuable!

1. *Hire the best, most experienced people you can.*

You need people who can help you anticipate problems and prevent them. And you need people who have developed their own internal "wisdom filter" through experience. The battle to get the best people for your project is the most important battle you can fight.

2. *Encourage team members to speak up and make themselves heard when they see something's going wrong.*

Chances are your team members will know about a looming problem for days before you'll hear about it. And if they feel free to let you in on it early you can often take action to fix it before things get out of control. (Just make sure they aren't simply complaining. Insist that they give you a suggestion for fixing things along with every complaint!)

3. *Do any menial work that's needed to keep your team moving.*

For example, when my team of tech writers was meeting with SMEs (subject matter experts) who would arrive without copies of documentation, I went to the copy center and made copies. Thus the team could conduct their interviews and still leave with reference material.

Generally, I like to think of myself as the guy in the white coveralls with a broom and garbage can, following the elephants in the parade. I locate the crap, deal with it, and help the marching band (my project team) avoid stepping in it so we can keep the music flowing.

4. Know your project life cycle cold.

At any point you should be able to tell any stakeholder or any project team member exactly what's going on, what's coming next, and what inputs they are expected to supply.

5. Continually sell the value of your project's systematic, iterative life cycle to sponsors and stakeholders.

Clients, contributing experts, and sometimes even team members themselves aren't always convinced that our project life cycles are made up of absolutely essential tasks. So it's up to you to make sure everyone knows that there's a bit of science behind your art. Convince them that your project's life cycle (i.e., its unique tasks, phases, reviews, revisions & iterations) are absolutely linked to the quality of your finished product. Make it clear that each review-revision loop is ultimately creating a solid foundation for success. (For more on project life cycles, see "Project Life Cycles versus Key PM Processes.")

6. Don't let your sponsors get out of making the tough decisions.

Sponsors usually engage project managers to create specific, tangible results. They typically don't hire project managers to determine their organizational priorities or strategic directions. Setting organizational priorities and strategies – and figuring out how these are manifested through specific project deliverables – is usually the sponsor's job. So make sure she does it! After all, that's why she's getting the "big bucks," right?

For example, if your team is building a new product, let the sponsor resolve the discrepancies between what the engineers say the product will be able to do and what the marketing people or lawyers say the product should do. It's simply not your job to resolve these kinds of disputes. In effect, you need to say to the sponsor: "Get back to me when you decide what you want this thing to do! We can make it do anything… you guys just need to figure out what you want!"

7. *Always create some sort of blueprint, design, flowchart, system specifications, outline, or other detailed "on paper" description of your finished product before you build the real thing.*

This way, people can review, argue over, revise and finalize these preliminary items before your team spends a lot of time (or invests a lot of creativity and passion) building your finished product. In other words, let them pick apart your choice of yarn before you spend the time and energy to knit an entire sweater – then have them reject it because it's the wrong color!

8. *Make sure your sponsors provide or, at the very least, approve all the experts on the team.*

After all, if your sponsors are paying for and approving your results, they should be prepared to stand behind the experts who will be helping you shape these results. If sponsors don't trust your experts, they'll likely spend a lot of time challenging your designs and your finished products. And that means you'll have to spend a lot of time and energy defending the experts' choices – or, worse, rebuilding your results to suit your sponsor's idiosyncratic vision of an expertly crafted finished product.

So at the very beginning of the project, before the finished results are described or designed, ask the sponsors to enlist the help of any experts they trust. And if they have no particular experts in mind, make sure your sponsors have a chance to meet, think about, and approve the experts you recommend.

9. *Protect your project team members.*

Make sure that everyone who is creating your project deliverables is protected from political disputes, unnecessary management reports, endless meetings, and low-value dog-and-pony shows. Handle these potential distractions yourself so the creators on your team can stay fresh and focus on making great contributions from their areas of expertise.

10. *Fight for enough time to do things right.*

If you cave in to ridiculous time demands and end up creating a lousy product, no one will remember how short the schedule was or how self-sacrificing you were when you agreed to it. They'll simply remember that you built something that is substandard. And the professionals who worked on your team will remember that they were frustrated because they had to cut corners, only to endure the disappointment of having built something that turned out to be second-rate. In either case, you're likely to end up with a client and team members who want nothing to do with you when it's time for that next project. So it's up to you to fight for (i.e., to defend the need for) enough time to do things right.

And what if they dig in their heels and won't allow you more time? Then try to negotiate to provide prototypes instead of finished products, provide solutions that are "buy-versus-build," or simply provide fewer items or fewer features than they originally wanted.

11. Know when to give in.

Don't lose the war because you couldn't resist fighting every little battle. As one of my more colorful senior managers used to say, "You don't wanna get in a pissing match unless you are ready to get wet!" So... ask yourself: "Is this really worth getting wet over?"

12. Understand that the brain is a physical mechanism that needs to be rested to work properly.

The brain is an electro-chemical mechanism whose neural synapses require periods of rest to prevent them from becoming clogged with waste products and malfunctioning (or maybe even going "blank," like you did in college, after pulling that "all-nighter" studying). So don't expect your highly-paid, well-educated, and creative professionals to produce quality results on a ridiculously short schedule. You wouldn't run a finely tuned race car without a pit stop, would you?!

13. Stay humble about your PM. And accept this in your heart: PM is overhead.

PM typically doesn't produce anything that end users need. Sure, PM can keep complicated team efforts coordinated and on track. But, in and of itself, PM doesn't create finished products. It creates its own sometimes-arcane artifacts (Gantt charts, budgets, network diagrams, etc.) that help managers up and down the food chain feel more confident. But PM doesn't create finished products.

So ask this question of everything you, in your role as project manager, do:

Is this really going to get my finished products done more quickly, with higher quality, and with less frustration on the part of those who are creating them?

If you ever answer "No" to this question then you should consider stopping that PM thing you are doing. It's fine for consultants and professional associations to suggest particular PM practices. Truth is, they want to sell you training and services to help you figure out the more complicated stuff! But unless these practices really improve your project results or make things better for your project team, you should feel free – maybe even feel obligated – to ignore the PM stuff as just so much overhead.

14. Step into the fear.

Know that at the beginning of nearly every project – especially when facing unfamiliar technical content – almost everyone experiences that moment when a little voice inside says, "I've finally done it! I'm really in over my head this time! This is where they find out I've been faking it! Aargh!"

When this voice speaks, remind yourself (or any team members who feel this fear) that you have heard this voice before and that you have a track record that says you will eventually overcome this fear, that you will soon resolve your confusion and you will succeed. Then use the energy of the fear to help you stay focused, alert, and resolved to get great results.

A couple of particularly good ways to deal with fear:

- Break down that which you fear into component parts or small steps. Then simply focus on addressing these one at a time.

- Find other people who have overcome the challenge you are facing. Ask them: How did they do it? What would they do differently? What was the most important thing they learned? What would they do if they were in your shoes?

- Then just step into the fear and do the next thing you know you must do to move you toward your project completion. Then do the next thing, and the next thing, and...

(See also this podcast, http://www.inspiredprojectteams.com/?p=645)

15. Be on the lookout for team members who are in pain and help them find ways to eliminate it.

All teams are different. And all project environments are different. But one thing's universal: When someone is frustrated, distraught, discouraged, or strung out so far he can't do his job properly, you can't ignore it. If you try to ignore it you might face an emotional meltdown or, less dramatically, end up with a team member who is producing inaccurate or haphazard work products. Either way, you shouldn't deny the reality of this person's pain. Your whole project could become a casualty of this neglect.

So when someone on your team is in misery, pause and try to find out more about what's causing the pain. Then think about the kinds of help or intervention the local culture will support. Finally, work within these local cultural boundaries to help him remove or reduce his pain and get back on track.

16. Think of yourself as a switchboard.

Constantly relay information and decisions to members of your project team. Keep everyone informed about what's going on with everyone else and the deliverables they are all creating. MBWA (Management by Walking Around) is a great way to gently and unobtrusively gather informal bits of information about the project's evolution and to share these. Remember: Creativity and quality often comes from the "cross pollination" of ideas that are shared among team members. And who better to quietly buzz around spreading the pollen of ideas than you, project manager?

17. *Fight for what's right.*

It's okay to feel a sense of righteous indignation and dig in your heals in the face of decisions that threaten the quality of your finished product. After all, no one will remember why you caved in to a half-assed work process or substandard tools or materials. They'll just know that your finished product is flawed. And so, too, will be your reputation and the reputation of the professionals on your team. More importantly, you will have spent your time and energy creating something that might not ever work the way people originally hoped it would work!

Now this isn't just about ego and professional standards. It's simply a stupid and short-sighted business practice to expend precious organizational resources (time, money, and peoples' effort) creating stuff that doesn't work right! But sometimes senior managers, especially those operating from a "Ready, Fire, Aim" frame of reference, ask professionals to do things that they themselves don't realize are stupid and short-sighted. So it's your role as a professional to "push back" and help senior management learn that they're asking for something dumb. In other words, one of your highest roles in the vast scheme of things is to fight for what's right!

18. *Insist that the sponsor (customer) sign off and approve deliverables as they are evolving.*

"You will pry my sign-offs out of my cold, dead hands!" – MG

Projects are finite. Projects must come to an end. Therefore our works-in-progress (our deliverables) must each come to an end. The question is: How can we know when we're done with that outline or that flow-chart or that set of design specifications? How do we know when we can confidently move on to the next iteration of our deliverables without having to go back and rethink or rework the stuff we ought to be finished with? The answer: Get a meaningful sign-off for each iteration of our deliverables. And that means getting the sponsor's signature to a statement indicating her approval of the work and agreeing that this hunk of work is now finalized... and we can now move on.

Make sure your sign-off includes some kind of consequences (more money, more time, or more resources) for completely rethinking a deliverable after it has been approved. After all, if your budget and schedule are limited, then the number of revisions must also be limited. That's only common sense... and it's only fair!

Think about it: Would you really expect a plumber whom you contracted to re-pipe your kitchen to expand the project and re-pipe your bathroom without charging you more and asking for more time? Of course not! So why let your sponsors get away with all sorts of add-ons without providing your team with more money and time. Aren't your team members as valuable as that plumber?

19. Develop a sense of humor and a "willful suspension of disbelief."

Things can't always make sense on a project. After all, we're working with humans who are often complicated mixes of weird histories, hidden agendas, and sometimes bizarre behaviors. And, unless something's diminishing the quality of your project outcomes, it's not always necessary that you fully understand all of the weirdness. There are times when it's easier, or at least more expeditious, to simply enjoy the ride.

In other words, when your customer is acting like Alice's Red Queen, then try to relax and enjoy the experience — The White Rabbit may be along soon and prove to be pleasant company!

20. Plan, plan, and re-plan.

The main work of a project manager is planning. Plan the marathon that is the project. Plan the sprints that are the activities and phases. Adjust the marathon strategy based on what happens during the sprints.

Use your own, organization-specific rules of thumb (project history) to lay the groundwork for a solid project plan. Then review that plan every week or so and revise it as needed. Remember that as the keeper of the plan, you should be constantly running ahead, just over the horizon, planting the flag and guiding your team to the next milestone.

FIVE ACTIONS THAT WILL HELP YOU SELL THAT COMPLICATED PROJECT

Let's face it. You wouldn't be a project manager if you fancied yourself a sales person. Indeed most project managers — particularly those who came up through the ranks of top project contributors and technical experts — hate all the "dog and pony show" stuff that's involved in selling their projects.

But the truth is there is simply no one who is in a better position to draw clear connecting lines between your team's amazing technical abilities and the value these bring to your organization through your project. What's more, as your project unfolds, you are going to need the enthusiastic support of senior management to help you get the money, people, facilities, equipment, and engaged participation of SMEs that will bring success. So it's up to you and the specific actions you take to build the sale and generate that much-needed senior management enthusiasm.

So where do you begin? Here are 5 actions that can help you sell your project to senior management:

1. Prove that you understand the business problem that is solved by your project.

Specifically, you need to explain (or better yet, demonstrate with evidence, ROI figures, etc.) how your deliverables will reduce your organization's pain, increase efficiency, save money, and have a tangible impact on making things better.

2. Show how each deliverable will add value.

Specifically, you need to make the connection between each item you will be creating and how it contributes to the value of the finished solution. (And no... you can't assume they can see these connections, just because they are obvious to you!) So you should quickly walk through your deliverables list and help the sponsor see how each is essential to the quality of the overall solution. This should include interim or draft deliverables like flow charts, scripts, first drafts, and so on. If possible, show models, mock-ups, demos, or anything that can make it real and generate that spark of enthusiasm that will keep your sponsor working on your behalf in the potentially difficult days ahead.

3. Connect the entire work process (including review/approval cycles) to quality.

In plain language, show how the work process is as lean as it can be, yet provides essential checks & balances (expert and managerial review, collaborative participation, etc.) that ensure quality. If appropriate, show how your work process is in sync with industry or competitors' "best practices."

4. Show how each member of your project team provides unique value.

Shine a light on the amazing expertise you've assembled and how each member of your team will make a unique contribution to the quality of the finished product. This is particularly important for team members who will eventually be asking the sponsor for access to key resources and other support as the project unfolds. It will really help if, when the team member knocks on that door to ask for help or feedback, that she will be doing so as a valuable "pre-sold" part of the project team.

5. Distinguish your project from apparently similar, but less complex or less valuable projects.

What's this mean? Simply this: Sponsors see and approve lots of projects. And before long they begin to see patterns in the ways that different kinds of projects unfold. Eventually they develop expectations about work processes and schedules that lead to similar types of deliverables.

Given these expectations, the more experienced and hard-nosed senior managers will almost always want to know your answer to this challenge: "I've seen similar project teams create similar outcomes using processes that were far less complicated. So why are you guys taking so long and going through so many cycles to achieve the same sorts of outcomes as Project XYZ?"

If you want to win the sale (and your sponsor's enthusiastic support) while hanging onto your best practices, you will need to have a good answer to this challenge!

Pulling It All Together: A Video Example

The video presentation in the link below, though it admittedly includes some ancient clip art, is a still-relevant example of how my team frequently answered sponsor challenges in order to sell our instructional development projects.

A little background: Most of our potential sponsors had substantial experience working with writers who created sales brochures, press releases, reports, etc. So many of these sponsors expected the process of developing training to be equivalent to the process of developing any written document. So, inevitably, such sponsors asked us these questions: "Why is your work process so complicated?... Why do you guys take so long?" This video shows how we answered these questions — and how I tried to implement the 5 actions outlined above.

*(Go to video: **Instructional Design Versus Message Design** at Vimeo — http://vimeo.com/53534224)*

STEP AWAY FROM THE COMPUTER AND GET OUT YOUR POST-IT NOTES!

All hands on deck!

A while back I was teaching an introductory PM class for some high-achieving tech folks. My overall goal was to begin to convert these perfectionists into project managers. Mid-way through the first morning, I divided the class into several small groups of 4 or 5 people and assigned a series of planning exercises. They had brought their own real world project ideas to class and the object of the game was to take a few of these from rough concept to full-blown, high-resolution project plans. Each team had been given large Post-It notes, blank flip charts, and markers. There were also a couple of white boards available.

As the teams were working through the guided planning exercises, I could hear the familiar jumble of voices as ideas were bounced around, discussed, discarded, and revised. One team, however, was strangely silent. Unlike the others who were up and moving about, they were seated around a table and looking at the back of one guy's computer screen. I walked over to see what was going on.

One member of this group had brought his laptop and was running MS Project. As I approached, he looked up from the keyboard and said, "I figured it would save a us lot of work later if we capture our ideas right now in Project. That way we won't have to transfer our notes from flip charts after we get back to the office. Okay?"

I paused and regarded him and his earnest fellow team members. They all seemed to be on board with this idea. So I said, "Sure. Go ahead and see how that works for you." I smiled encouragingly, left them to their work and went on to observe the other teams.

Watch Out for the Quiet Ones

As the day unfolded the teams worked their way through the assigned planning exercises. First they created deliverables (WBS) lists, then task/activity lists, then time estimates and finally schedules. At the end of each exercise a spokesperson for each team would present their team's results for evaluation by the rest of the class. Overall, it was a typical class. Or was it?

Something was weird about the laptop-driven team. During the debriefings, the guy who had been inputting data into MS Project was always the spokesperson. In fact, he did all the talking! In contrast, the other teams would rotate spokespersons and almost all the members would chime in at random during the debriefings.

I also noticed that during the assignments, while the other teams were moving around, taking turns at the flip chart or white board, sharing the chore of writing the Post Its, etc., the laptop-driven team was far more quiet and inactive. The guy at the keyboard, however, was intensely focused on his work. His fellow team members would add a thought here and there and he would type something in response and read it back to them. Most of them couldn't see the computer screen. They seemed to trust that he was capturing their ideas accurately.

As the day wore on, it became clear that the laptop-driven team really had only one person in charge — one owner — one person who was in control of both the big picture and how all the pieces fit together! And in sharp contrast to the flip chart, Post-It driven teams, who were often noisy and contentious, these folks were quite subdued. It was clear to me that they simply didn't care as much about this project. And, to be honest, their project solution was ultimately less creative than the others'.

It's Gotta Be "Our Project," Not "My Project!"

So what's the lesson here? Simply this. While technology like MS Project can contribute powerfully to the ongoing monitoring and management of a project, it can be like a straight-jacket during project conceptualization. When team members engage an old-fashioned flip chart or wall full of Post It notes, they're free to quickly scribble ideas, underline some and cross out others. It's messy, nonthreatening and, above all, democratic. And when a team studies a wall full of hand-drawn notes, it's clear they're working with an unfinished, unpolished product. So it feels okay to jump in with additions and changes. The result: everyone feels equally empowered to step up, grab a marker, post a note, and engage the project concepts.

At the same time, because you're dealing with tangible, physical objects, the process is active and kinesthetically engaging. The between-the-lines message of all this activity is: We're a team... this is *our* project. And if they are all going to stay motivated once the project is up and running, they must feel this empowerment and ownership right from the start.

Contrast this with how the laptop-driven team must have felt after leaving those planning sessions. Those folks who were simply contributing voices could walk away with far less commitment to the project. After all, Keyboard Guy had captured it all anyway. It was his problem now, right?

So Step Away from the Computer...

So the next time you find yourself cranking up the latest PM software in the presence of your core team, stakeholders, or contributors — and especially if you're in the early days of the project — ask yourself these questions:

- Can everyone in this group see what's on my screen?

- Is everyone equally empowered to act on this software and see their input become part of the project concept?

- By using this tool, am I really inviting group participation? If not, why am I using it in a group setting?

It's not just about manipulating the situation and getting "buy in." It's about inviting all team members to authentically engage, reach out and embrace the project by ensuring their voices are heard and their concepts are fairly processed.

In short, **it's about making sure it's Our Project and not simply My Project!** And the best way to do this during project conceptualization is to step away from the computer and get out your Post It notes and flip charts.

KEEPING THINGS MOVING: A "TO DO" LIST TO HELP YOU EXECUTE, CONTROL, AND CLOSE OUT YOUR PROJECT

Instructions: After your project plan is approved and you are up and running, you can use the checklist below and related items to help you keep things moving according to your plan. Go through this list at least weekly for each project you are managing.

Check Your Project's Scope.

Refresh your memory about your project's goals and boundaries. In particular, make sure you have a clear picture of what the desired results should be at this point relative to deliverables, schedule costs, quality, and so on.

(See Worksheet: Project Scope Statement* under Action Item: Describe Project Scope if you don't already have a formal scope statement.*)

Check Your Deliverables.

Analyze the status of each project deliverable. Are they evolving as planned? If appropriate:

- Locate lists of quality criteria that may be applied to inspect the quality and completeness of the deliverables at this stage of the project.

- Check contractors' proposals or contracts to make sure you know what they should be supplying at this point.

- Inspect all project deliverables.
- Decide whether to accept inspected deliverables or to require rework.

(See Worksheet: Project Deliverables Status Analyzer.*)

Check Your Schedule.

- Examine your milestones, key dates, and critical path. Are you where you need to be?

Analyze Variances (Deviations from Plan) by Comparing "Estimated" to "Actual."

- Are activities taking longer than planned? (Are you exceeding estimates of duration?)
- Are you using more resource hours than you planned?
- Are your actual costs exceeding your estimated costs?
- If minor variances are discovered (variances that can be resolved easily without changing the plan or scope), then resolve them.
- If major variances are discovered (variances that change the scope or constitute significant project issues), then handle them as described in the steps below.

(See Worksheet: Variance Analyzer.*)

Address Scope Changes.

- Identify changes in scope (changes in deliverables, schedule, costs, etc.).
- Handle scope changes, if necessary.

(See Guidelines: Handling Scope Change* and Worksheet: Project Scope Change Order.*)

List, Track, and Try to Resolve Open Issues.

- Make a list of all the unresolved issues, or
- Revisit the list of open issues from the last inspection period and try to resolve them.

(See Worksheet: Project Issue Tracker.*)

Revisit Potential Project Risks.

- Locate the Risk Management Plan, if one has been created.
- Note particularly whether any of the ongoing events or upcoming events are identified in the risk management plan as particularly vulnerable to risk.

Report Project Status.

- After completing the checks above, if you haven't already done so, talk to your team members and determine their perspective on project status.
- Create and circulate a project status report.

(See Worksheet: The Project Status Report.*)

Drive for Close-Out of Activities and Sign-off of Deliverables as Appropriate.

- Ask yourself, "What activities can I close out? Which deliverables can I get formally approved and signed-off?"
- Prepare and get signatures on sign-off forms as appropriate.

(See Worksheet: Sample Project Sign-off Form* under Action Item: Close Out Project Activities.*)

Decide Whether It's Appropriate to Kill the Project Then Do So, If Necessary.

(See Appendix E: Guidelines—When to Kill the Project.*)

Create a List of Lessons Learned.

- Create a list of lessons learned that describes the ways subsequent project activities must be modified in order to prevent the difficulties encountered up to this point.

- Complete Appropriate Evaluation Checklists.

- Complete evaluation checklists, if applicable, and file them as part of the official project records.

** This item is located in **The Project Management Minimalist** and/or **The Project Manager's Partner** by Michael Greer. If you don't have either of those books, you can email me at pm.minimalist@gmail.com and tell me which worksheet you'd like to see. I'll send it to you. – Mike G.*

14 KEY PRINCIPLES FOR PM SUCCESS

(This is an excerpt from Michael Greer's "Chapter 6: Planning and Managing Human Performance Technology Projects," **Handbook of Human Performance Technology, San Francisco, Jossey-Bass, 1999)**

1. **Project managers must focus on three dimensions of project success.** Simply put, project success means completing all project deliverables on **time**, within **budget**, and to a level of **quality** that is acceptable to sponsors and stakeholders. The project manager must keep the team's attention focused on achieving these broad goals.

2. **Planning is everything — and ongoing.** On one thing all PM texts and authorities agree: The single most important activity that project managers engage in is planning — detailed, systematic, team-involved plans are the only foundation for project success. And when real-world events conspire to change the plan, project managers must make a new one to reflect the changes. So planning and replanning must be a way of life for project managers.

3. **Project managers must feel, and transmit to their team members, a sense of urgency.** Because projects are finite endeavors with limited time, money, and other resources available, they must be kept moving toward completion. Since most team members have lots of other priorities, it's up to the project manager to keep their attention on project deliverables and deadlines. Regular status checks, meetings, and reminders are essential.

4. **Successful projects use a time-tested, proven project life cycle**. We know what works. Models such as the standard ISD model and others described in this text can help ensure that professional standards and best practices are built into our project plans. Not only do these models typically support quality, they help to minimize rework. So when time or budget pressures seem to encourage taking short cuts, it's up to the project manager to identify and defend the best project life cycle for the job.

5. **All project deliverables and all project activities must be visualized and communicated in vivid detail.** In short, the project manager and project team must early on create a tangible picture of the finished deliverables in the minds of everyone involved so that all effort is focused in the same direction. Avoid vague descriptions at all costs; spell it out, picture it, prototype it, and make sure everyone agrees to it.

6. **Deliverables must evolve gradually, in successive approximations.** It simply costs too much and risks too much time spent in rework to jump in with both feet and begin building all project deliverables. Build a little at a time, obtain incremental reviews and approvals, and maintain a controlled evolution.

7. **Projects require clear approvals and sign-off by sponsors.** Clear approval points, accompanied by formal sign-off by sponsors, SMEs, and other key stakeholders, should be demarcation points in the evolution of project deliverables. It's this simple: anyone who has the power to reject or to demand revision of deliverables after they are complete must be required to examine and approve them as they are being built.

8. **Project success is correlated with thorough analyses of the need for project deliverables.** Our research has shown that when a project results in deliverables that are designed to meet a thoroughly documented need, then there is a greater likelihood of project success. So managers should insist that there is a

documented business need for the project before they agree to consume organizational resources in completing it.

9. **Project managers must fight for time to do things right.** In our work with project managers we often hear this complaint: "We always seem to have time to do the project over; I just wish we had taken the time to do it right in the first place!" Projects must have available enough time to "do it right the first time." And project managers must fight for this time by demonstrating to sponsors and top managers why it's necessary and how time spent will result in quality deliverables.

10. **Project manager responsibility must be matched by equivalent authority.** It's not enough to be held responsible for project outcomes; project managers must ask for and obtain enough authority to execute their responsibilities. Specifically, managers must have the authority to acquire and coordinate resources, request and receive SME cooperation, and make appropriate, binding decisions which have an impact on the success of the project.

11. **Project sponsors and stakeholders must be active participants, not passive customers.** Most project sponsors and stakeholders rightfully demand the authority to approve project deliverables, either wholly or in part. Along with this authority comes the responsibility to be an active participant in the early stages of the project (helping to define deliverables), to complete reviews of interim deliverables in a timely fashion (keeping the project moving), and to help expedite the project manager's access to SMEs, members of the target audience, and essential documentation.

12. **Projects typically must be sold, and resold.** There are times when the project manager must function as salesperson to maintain the commitment of stakeholders and sponsors. With project plans in hand, project managers may need to periodically

remind people about the business need that is being met and that their contributions are essential to help meet this need.

13. **Project managers should acquire the best people they can and then do whatever it takes to keep the garbage out of their way.** By acquiring the best people — the most skilled, the most experienced, the best qualified — the project manager can often compensate for too little time or money or other project constraints. Project managers should serve as an advocate for these valuable team members, helping to protect them from outside interruptions and helping them acquire the tools and working conditions necessary to apply their talents.

14. **Top management must actively set priorities.** In today's leaner, self-managing organizations, it is not uncommon for project team members to be expected to play active roles on many project teams at the same time. Ultimately, there comes a time when resources are stretched to their limits and there are simply too many projects to be completed successfully. In response, some organizations have established a Project Office comprised of top managers from all departments to act as a clearinghouse for projects and project requests. The Project Office reviews the organization's overall mission and strategies, establishes criteria for project selection and funding, monitors resource workloads, and determines which projects are of high enough priority to be approved. In this way top management provides the leadership necessary to prevent multi-project log jams. *(See also "Chapter 40, What's Project Portfolio Management (PPM) and Why Should Project Managers Care About It?")*

PROJECT LIFE CYCLES VERSUS KEY PM PROCESSES

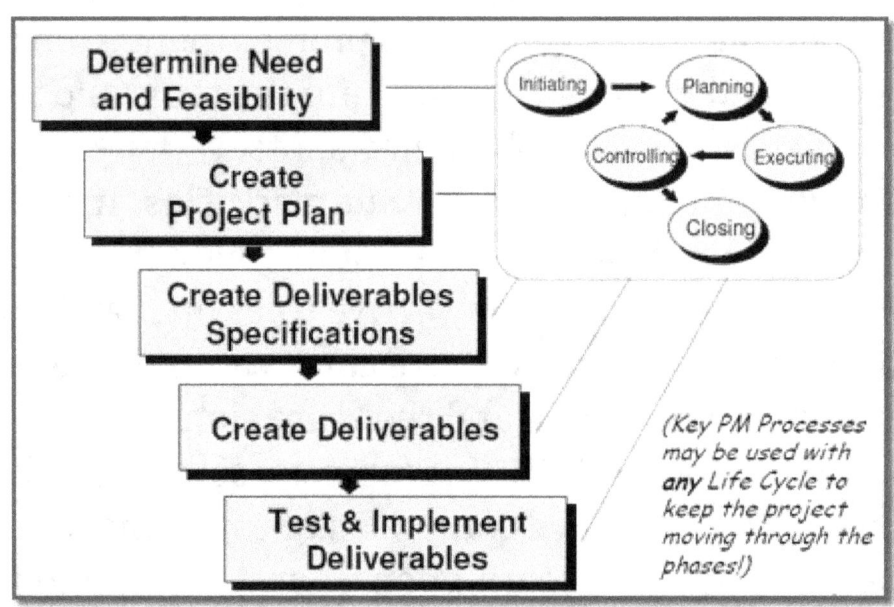

A Sample Project Life Cycle & The 5 Essential PM Processes

We know that **a project life cycle is made up of a collection of related phases. And each phase in the life cycle is made up of a bunch of related tasks or activities.** And the exact nature of all these tasks, activities, and phases is dependent entirely upon the finished products (deliverables) you are trying to create. So, a media producer has a "Scripting" phase made up of many tasks related to drafting and refining the script. And a home builder has a "Blueprint" phase made up of creating and refining the home's floor plans. And a software developer has a "Design" phase in which clear software specifications are created to guide the programmers. You get the idea: **Deliverables determine**

the tasks & activities needed, which in turn determine the project life cycle.

In the graphic above, **the blue boxes on the left show a generic project life cycle** (organized as a "waterfall" project structure*) which can be used to create almost any type of finished product.

On the other hand, there are the **Five Key PM Processes** (represented by the yellow bubbles in the diagram above) that pretty much everyone agrees are universal: Initiate, Plan, Execute, Control, and Close Out. No matter what your project, you can apply these processes to keep things moving.

The trouble is that a lot of PM newbies (and organizations who are new to PM) confuse the five generic PM processes with their life cycles. They try to pound the square pegs of their project's necessarily unique phases into the round holes that are the five generic PM processes.

The result is that I sometimes find myself working with clients who insist that their local PM model has a distinct phase labeled "Plan" or "Execute" or, worse yet, "Control." But, I usually ask them, how can you possibly restrict all "execution" chores to a single phase? And aren't you "controlling" throughout the project? As you can see, this can all be very confusing for a PM newcomer.

Though it usually takes some time to sink in, here's my bottom line message to these folks: **Any project's life cycle (that collection of tasks, activities, and phases) is unique and always reflect a specific set of deliverables or "best practices" of an industry. On the other hand, any project's work processes (i.e., what you do to move from phase to phase) involves the 5 generic PM processes: Initiate, Plan, Execute, Control, and Close-Out.** So no matter what phase of a project you're in (any project!), you must Initiate that phase, then Plan that phase (or revisit & revise the Plan), Execute the tasks associated with that phase, Control the tasks, and finally Close Out that phase. When you complete the phase (i.e., when you "close out" the phase), then you start all over again with the next phase and Initiate, Plan (replan), Execute/Control, and Close Out that phase. And so it goes... over and over again.

Some Videos & a PDF to Help Clarify

As a PM trainer I've spent considerable time helping people get this important distinction straight. To help clarify, I've created these videos:

- **Video 2-B: PM Nuts & Bolts (from my "Become a Project Management Minimalist" video series –** http://michaelgreer.biz/?p=930 **)** discusses project life cycles and how they should reflect your unique deliverables and how these life cycles should shape your planning efforts. The video includes several real-life examples.

- **A Zillion Project Management Models & Why You Should Build Another One!** (Find it on my General Project Management Playlist on YouTube: https://www.youtube.com/user/greerspm/playlists)

- **A PM Minimalist's Perspective on Agile, Scrum, & Waterfall** (http://vimeo.com/channels/michaelgreer/27089817)

The link below is from a PDF file of a few slides I sometimes share with PM-newbie clients to help them see the distinction (and the relationship) between the Five Key PM Processes and their project's unique life cycle. Click the link, check them out, provide your own narration, and maybe you can help clarify this confusing topic for a PM newbie you know!

- **PDF of Slides: Life Cycles versus Key PM Processes** (http://michaelgreer.biz/sample-life-cycles-and-key-pm-processes.pdf)

BEYOND WORDS: THE POWER OF "MAKING IT REAL" TO INSPIRE AND FOCUS EFFORT

One of the toughest, but most mission-critical, responsibilities of a project manager is to get people excited about the project before there is anything to show. We ask potential champions to engage and connect with something that isn't yet real — something that exists as a concept only. Once they "buy in" and become enthusiastic, they can rally the support of their colleagues, help to pull together project funding and open the doors to key SMEs and gatekeepers. But how can we inspire support for a non-existent finished product?

In my early days as an instructional developer for a large consulting firm, one of our best sales reps explained the situation to me: "You realize, don't you, that we're just selling poof-balls and mumbly-dust!? We come in with our 25-page proposal that is really nothing but ink characters on paper and we ask them to sign a $100,000 contract. And we ask them to trust that we'll make something real and useful from that collection of pages. To tell you the truth, I'm amazed we're able to sell any projects at all!"

Poof-Balls and Mumbly Dust!

And he was right! Closing sales required gargantuan leaps of faith on the part of our potential clients. And since most of the client decision-makers were smart business people, we had to figure out how to move beyond the "poof-balls and mumbly dust" and help them make a meaningful connection with our "castles in the air." So how did we do it?

The truth is, it didn't involve any alchemy or sleight of hand. We simply did what food sellers, car dealers, book publishers and real estate people had been doing successfully for years: We found a way to let them sample what we were hoping to sell them. The result is that they didn't need to make a huge leap of faith. Instead, they could come to understand, up close and personally, what we had planned for them. And this reduced the perceived risk (the risk of their betting on the unknown) so they could relax and make their "go or no go" decision more easily.

Here are **a few ways we helped them sample our proposed solutions:**

- Show them a portion of a similar finished product that we produced for another client.

- Connect them with an enthusiastic user who was successfully working with a similar finished product.

- Create a customized mockup using a small portion of their proprietary content.

- Run a small prototype training session that employed the key elements of the proposed solution so they could feel the course flow and dynamics that would be involved.

You Gotta Make It Real!

Like a food seller giving samples in the grocery store, a car dealer giving test drives, a book publisher giving away the first chapter of a book or a real estate developer walking potential buyers through a model unit, we "made it real." Often this deeper level of knowing helped us flush out objections so they could be addressed and quickly laid to rest. Sometimes we were able to stimulate a constructive dialogue about how to enhance our proposed solution so that it would better fit their needs. In the end, they came to "know" what they were getting into before they signed the contract. And, through this knowing, they would often develop their own enthusiasm, becoming internal evangelists for the project and making our sales effort all the easier.

A Clear, Compelling Target: Come and Get It!

Some say that it was President Kennedy's vision of a mission to the moon that in 1961 inspired a generation of US scientists and engineers to develop breakthrough aerospace materials and methods that had never before existed. Indeed, JFK is credited with harnessing the talents of hundreds of thousands of people whose focused efforts achieved the July 1969 moon landing.

While there's no doubt about Kennedy's power to inspire, I like to think that it was also the moon itself, peering down at us from 239,000 miles away — taunting us — daring us to take that leap across the spatial void that ultimately "made it real" for all those scientists and engineers. And once this silvery-white target was burned into their mind's eye, there was no stopping them.

So what about you? What do you need to "make real" for your team or your sponsor in order to trigger their enthusiastic engagement? How can you give them a spicy taste of the future you want them to build? **As all the best sales reps know, if you want to inspire passion, you'll need to go beyond words and make it real!**

FORMAL, WRITTEN SIGN OFF: A SIMPLE AND POWERFUL PM TOOL

A few years ago I was contracted to build a two-week long technical course for a major high-tech client. A fairly large effort, our project's finished deliverables included self-study materials, job aids, studio-produced video case study scenarios and instructor guides — in short, we were building a complete, integrated training system with a lot of moving parts. My team of independent contractors consisted of five training developers (instructional designers), a print production coordinator and a video production subcontractor.*

After several difficult weeks of interviewing the client's in-house SMEs, gathering information, brainstorming and welding together a cohesive course design, we rolled out our first major deliverable, our Blueprint (an integrated training design plan). My contract stipulated that our Blueprint would be formally approved by the client, in writing, before we moved on to the next phase, which would be developing our fully fleshed-out first drafts of all materials and video scripts.

Love Is In The Air! ... Maybe ...

On Blueprint approval day we sat down with our client project representative, a big, friendly bear of a guy who had been truly supportive of all our efforts. One by one each designer presented his or her portion of the Blueprint, while the video producer presented the treatments for the matching scenarios. The client was delighted! After each team member's presentation, he praised their work, noting his appreciation of specific challenges they had overcome or creative leaps they had made. It was a project manager's dream! Love was in the air!

At the end of the day the contractors were each sent home with a hug and a pat on the back. And there we sat... just the two of us. Beaming, my client told me how I should be really proud of my team and how he was looking forward to seeing the course come alive in the next iteration. In turn, I told him how much we appreciated his stalwart support throughout.

Still smiling and feeling confident, I reached into my briefcase and pulled out my Blueprint Sign-Off form. It stated 1) that the client approved our Blueprint in its entirety, as presented, and 2) the the client understood that any further changes, additions or deletions to our design could result in increased costs (i.e., more fees billed) and schedule extensions. And at the bottom of the form was a big blank space for the client's written signature, just above his clearly printed name and job title.

Actually... A Chill Is In the Air!

Studying the form, my client's smile faded. When he finished reading he laid it down in front of him, placed both hands on the table and sat up straight. His brow became furrowed and his jaw muscles clenched a couple of times. The love that had been in the air was replaced by a slight chill and a cool silence.

Finally, he spoke, "I can't do it, Mike. I'm sorry. The engineers are still making some changes that could ripple through most of the training design. And the guys at legal still haven't approved two of the video scenarios."

I swallowed hard. This was a big contract and I didn't want to lose it. On the other hand, I was paying each of my team members a lot of money and I couldn't afford to pay them extra for "do-overs." Besides, as first-rate independent contractors they had each scheduled other projects when they completed this one. They certainly couldn't wait around while the client's stakeholders delayed their decisions. Sighing (and trying to ignore my heart pounding in my ears) I told my client all this. Then I said, "I'm sorry. But unless you can get these issues resolved and give me a formal approval for this phase, I'm gonna have to release my team. I can wait a couple of days, but after that I've got to cut them loose." He nodded slowly and said he understood. Then I went home.

That night I was really scared. I had cleared my schedule for this big project, so nothing else was in my hopper. Worse, I had to call each of the team members and tell them to stop work until they heard from me. What a nasty conclusion to an otherwise triumphant day!

A Crystallizing Moment

Late the next afternoon my phone rang. My client was on the line and he informed me that he had been able to get clear, "semi-final" specs from the engineers and these didn't seem to impact our design substantially. In addition, he had got the approval on the video scenarios from legal. So he would sign my Blueprint approval the next morning and the project could continue on schedule. Whew! We had dodged a bullet on that one!

Almost a decade (and many shared projects) later, I attended a holiday party with this client. Warmed by the glow of the season and a couple of cups of holiday cheer, we were reminiscing about some of the challenges we had overcome together. I recalled that fateful (and truly scary!) moment when I had walked out of his office without my Blueprint Sign-Off, leaving him facing a potential project cancellation.

I said, "Man... I hated doing that. But the contract called for formal Sign-Off , so..."

He interrupted me, looked me straight in the eyes and chuckled, "Mike, I gotta tell you that was the best thing you could have done. When you did that, you empowered me to go back to those guys and tell them the project was now on hold and that it was time to get off their butts and make some decisions! I made it clear to them that they were the ones who'd be blamed for bringing down the whole project. So it was great! The formal Sign-Off forced us to get all our stuff resolved."

Wow! I suddenly felt like I had simply been an actor in a big play. And by courageously playing my part, as scripted, I helped move the plot forward toward a sensible conclusion.

Lesson Learned

The lesson I learned here: There is a **huge** difference between verbal approval and formal, written approval via a legal signature. Though words of praise and approval may be accompanied by smiles, handshakes and hugs, they are still simply ephemeral sounds and gestures that evaporate without a trace.

On the other hand, when clients, sponsors, customers or SMEs pick up a pen and write a personal signature, it is not only a kinesthetic event, but a public and lasting declaration — on the record — that they stand firmly behind their decisions. In this way a formal, written Sign-Off can be a powerful, crystallizing moment in a project's evolution.

So these days I tell the PM newbies in my classes, "You will have to pry my Sign-Off out of my cold, dead hands!" A little too dramatic? Perhaps. But you'll never catch me working without these powerful, energy-shifting tools.

_____

* The events as described here are 90% accurately recalled. Some details may have been distorted by the years, but it's mostly a true story.

REWORK WILL HAPPEN! SO DON'T BE AMBUSHED. BUILD IT IN.

In my classes, I like to tell my students that stakeholders are like new puppies in the backyard: They gotta mark their territory and leave their scent on everything they see! They need to make the project deliverables their own by adjusting them, changing them, reinterpreting them, and otherwise "branding" them with their own perspectives.

In other words, if they are doing what you want them to do — actively engaging with your team and with your project's deliverables as they are evolving — they are absolutely guaranteed to make modifications and adjustments as they begin to "own" the project's outputs. And that's a good thing! You want this kind of ownership to help assure the success of your project's finished work products when they are finally turned over to the users.

The down side of this, however, is that it leads to rework as you make all the suggested revisions.

The **key question** for you, as project manager, is this:

- **Will you accommodate this stakeholder-generated rework by formally building it into the project plan or will you simply be ambushed by it when the stakeholders surprise you with all their divergent feedback at your review sessions?**

Never Build More Than You Want to Revise

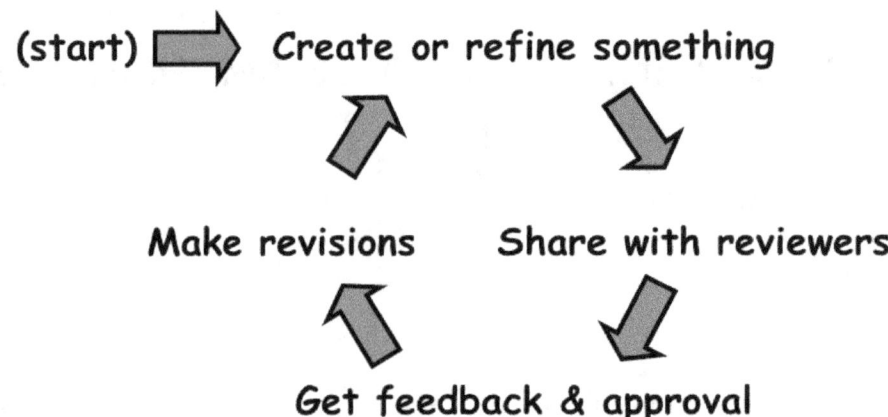

Build/create a little at a time!

The spirit of the diagram above is this: ***Never build more than you want to spend time revising***. That is, don't risk hours of work in the "wrong" direction.

Get feedback early and make adjustments early, then repeat — a little at a time, in small increments.

How to Design a Project with Rework Opportunities Built In

The following process (from my Book, ***The Project Management Minimalist***, "Step 4: Figure out what you need to do to complete the work products.") will guide you through the process of designing a project plan with plenty of rework built in.

1. **Assemble all project documentation you've created so far,** including the stakeholder-approved Project Scope Statement, WBS (work breakdown structure), technical specifications, proposals, and so on.

2. **Assemble the core project team and as many stakeholders as possible.**

3. **Conduct a brainstorming session** in which the core project team and stakeholders do the following:

- Examine each specific deliverable that must be created. (Refer to your WBS...)

- List the specific tasks that must be performed to cause that deliverable to evolve from rough idea to finished product. (Use yellow stickies, flip charts, white boards, mind mapping methodology and other tools of brainstorming you like.)

- Incorporate plenty of opportunities for stakeholders to review work products in small increments, as they are evolving. So, for example, if you are writing a report, don't wait until you're finished to share it with reviewers. Instead, share (and get feedback and make revisions to) an outline first and then a rough draft, before you spend your time finalizing and polishing the report. Specifically, insert as many "create, share, feedback, revise" cycles into your task list as possible. This will help prevent unplanned rework (and blown schedules from having stakeholders reject your deliverables!) by building opportunities for review and revision into your plan.

- Combine and organize the list of tasks/activities into broad collections of related tasks or phases.

- Create a network diagram (flow chart) showing the sequence and flow of all project tasks, activities, and phases.

4. **Polish and finalize the network diagram and task list.**

5. **Circulate the network diagram and task list to appropriate stakeholders/sponsor and get formal approval (i.e., sign-off).**

Like Puppies in the Yard

Remember, your project stakeholders are like new puppies in the backyard: They need to mark territory! They need to make the project deliverables their own by adjusting them, changing them, reinterpreting them, and otherwise "branding" them with their own perspectives. Work with your stakeholders, using the steps outlined above, to create a shared set of project steps that allows them plenty of opportunity to shape the deliverables systematically, in a scheduled and fully-anticipated fashion. This way you won't be ambushed by a pile of unanticipated changes that blow your project schedule and budget!

PROJECT "POST MORTEM" REVIEW QUESTIONS

Overview

It's important for project managers and team members to take stock at the end of a project and develop a list of lessons learned so that they don't repeat their mistakes in the next project. Typically such reviews are called post-project reviews or "post mortems." I recommend a **two-step process** for conducting these reviews:

1. **First, prepare and circulate a whole bunch of specific questions** about the project and give team members time to think about them and prepare their responses individually.
2. **Next, hold a meeting and discuss the team's responses** to the questions. The result of this discussion is often a list of "Lessons Learned."

The benefit of the first step, done individually by team members, is that it allows the quieter, more analytical people to develop their responses to the questions without being interrupted by the more outgoing, vocal types who might otherwise dominate in the face-to-face meeting. Also, it allows everyone the time to create more thoughtful responses.

So what would be on the list of questions? I've provided some of my favorites below.

General Questions

1. Are you proud of our finished deliverables (project work products)? If yes, what's so good about them? If no, what's wrong with them?
2. What was the single most frustrating part of our project?
3. How would you do things differently next time to avoid this frustration?
4. What was the most gratifying or professionally satisfying part of the project?
5. Which of our methods or processes worked particularly well?
6. Which of our methods or processes were difficult or frustrating to use?
7. If you could wave a magic wand and change anything about the project, what would you change?
8. Did our stakeholders, senior managers, customers, and sponsor(s) participate effectively? If not, how could we improve their participation?

Phase-Specific Questions

(These will differ from project to project, depending on the life cycle/ phases. The phases identified below are explained in detail in ***The Project Management Minimalist: Just Enough PM to Rock Your Projects!)***

Phase I: Determine Need and Feasibility

1. Did our needs/market analysis or feasibility study identify all the project deliverables that we eventually had to build? If not, what did we miss and how can we be sure our future analyses don't miss such items?
2. Did our needs/market analysis or feasibility study identify unnecessary deliverables? If so, how can we be sure our future analyses don't make this mistake?

3. How could we have improved our need-feasibility or analysis phase?

Phase II: Create Project Plan

1. How accurate were our original estimates of the size and effort of our project? What did we over or under estimate? (Consider deliverables, work effort, materials required, etc.)
2. How could we have improved our estimate of size and effort so that it was more accurate?
3. Did we have the right people assigned to all project roles? (Consider subject matter expertise, technical contributions, management, review and approval, and other key roles) If no, how can we make sure that we get the right people next time.
4. Describe any early warning signs of problems that occurred later in the project? How should we have reacted to these signs? How can we be sure to notice these early warning signs next time?
5. Could we have completed this project without one or more of our vendors/contractors? If so, how?
6. Were our constraints, limitations, and requirements made clear to all vendors/contractors from the beginning? If not, how could we have improved our RFP or statement of need?
7. Were there any difficulties negotiating the vendor contract? How could these have been avoided?
8. Were there any difficulties setting up vendor paperwork (purchase orders, contracts, etc.) or getting the vendor started? How could these have been avoided?
9. List team members or stakeholders who were missing from the kickoff meeting or who were not involved early enough in our project. How can we avoid these oversights in the future?
10. Were all team/stakeholder roles and responsibilities clearly delineated and communicated? If not, how could we have improved these?

11. Were the deliverables specifications, milestones, and specific schedule elements/dates clearly communicated? If not, how could we improve this?

Phase III: Create Specifications for Deliverables

1. Were you proud of our blueprints or other detailed design specifications? If not, how could we have improved these?
2. Did all the important project players have creative input into the creation of the design specifications? If not, who were we missing and how can we assure their involvement next time?
3. Did those who reviewed the design specifications provide timely and meaningful input? If not, how could we have improved their involvement and the quality of their contributions?
4. How could we have improved our work process for creating deliverables specifications?
5. [Insert your own, deliverables-specific questions here.]

Phase IV: Create Deliverables

- Were you proud of our deliverables? If not, how could we have improved these?

- Did all the important project players have creative input into the creation of the deliverables? If not, who were we missing and how can we assure their involvement next time?

- Did those who reviewed the deliverables provide timely and meaningful input? If not, how could we have improved their involvement and the quality of their contributions?

- How could we have improved our work process for creating deliverables?

- [Insert your own, deliverables-specific questions here.]

Phase V: Test and Implement Deliverables

1. Were the members of our test audience truly representative of our target audience? If not, how could we assure better representation in the future?
2. Did the test facilities, equipment, materials, and support people help to make the test an accurate representation of how the deliverables will be used in the "real world?" If not, how could we have improved on these items?
3. Did we get timely, high-quality feedback about how we might improve our deliverables? If not, how could we get better feedback in the future?
4. Was our implementation strategy accurate and effective? How could we improve this strategy?
5. Did our hand-off of deliverables to the user/customer/sponsor represent a smooth and easy transition? If not, how could we have improved this process?
6. [Insert your own, deliverables-specific questions here.]

Note: This tool is from my book, ***The Project Management Minimalist: Just Enough PM to Rock Your Projects!*** It's also available as a free PDF at my website.

TEN GUARANTEED WAYS TO SCREW UP ANY PROJECT

1. **Don't bother prioritizing your organization's overall project load.** After all, if there's a free-for-all approach to your overall program management (i.e., "survival of the fittest"), then the projects that survive will be those that were destined to survive. In the meantime, senior management need not trouble themselves aligning projects with strategic goals or facing the logical imperative that people simply cannot have 12 number one priorities! (See my online article *What's Project Portfolio Management (PPM) and Why Should Project Managers Care About It?*)
2. **Encourage sponsors and key stakeholders to take a passive role on the project team.** Let them assert their authority to reject deliverables at random, without participating in defining project outcomes in a high-resolution fashion. And above all, don't bother project sponsors when their constituents (such as key SMEs and reviewers) drop the ball and miss their deadlines.
3. **Set up ongoing committees focusing on management process** (such as TQM groups, etc.) and make project team members participate in frequent meetings and write lots of reports... preferably when critical project deadlines are coming due.
4. **Interrupt team members relentlessly** ... preferably during their time off. Find all sorts of trivial issues that "need to be addressed," then keep their cell phones ringing and bury them in emails to keep them off balance.
5. **Create a culture in which project managers are expected to**

"roll over" and take it when substantive new deliverables are added halfway through the project. (After all, only a tradesperson like a plumber or electrician would demand more money or more time for additional services; our people are "professionals" and should be prepared to be "flexible.")

6. **Half way through the project,** when most of the deliverables have begun to take shape, **add a whole bunch of previously unnamed stakeholders** and ask them for their opinions about the project and its deliverables.

7. Encourage the sponsor to approve deliverables informally (with nods, smiles, and verbal praise); **never force sponsors to stand behind their approvals with a formal sign-off.** (In other words, give 'em plenty of room to weasel out of agreements!)

8. **Make sure project managers have lots of responsibilities and deadlines, but no authority** whatsoever to acquire or remove people from the project; to get enough money, materials, or facilities; or insist on timely participation of SMEs and key reviewers.

9. **Describe project deliverables in the vaguest possible terms** so sponsors and reviewers have plenty of leeway to reinvent the project outputs repeatedly as the project unfolds.

10. **Get projects up and running as quickly as possible** – don't worry about documenting agreements in a formal project charter, clearly describing team roles/responsibilities, or doing a thorough work breakdown analysis. After all, we know what we're doing and we trust each other. So let's get to it without a pesky audit trail!

SUMMARY: 10 STEPS TO PROJECT SUCCESS

*(Note: This summary is from my book, **The Project Management Minimalist: Just Enough PM to Rock Your Projects!**, which provides a thorough explanation of each step, as well as tools, worksheets, etc. to help complete the step. This summary is also available as a single-page PDF reference table at my website. Please email pm.minimalist@gmail.com for samples of any items referenced here)*

1. Define the project concept, then get support and approval.

Results of Successful Performance:

- A series of conversations, brainstorming sessions, and other formal or informal discussions about the project concept with your supervisor and key people whom you hope will provide project support

- An approved Project Charter

2. Get your team together and start the project.

Results of Successful Performance:

- A series of conversations, brainstorming sessions, and other formal/ informal discussions about the project concept with all stakeholders

- Commitments from stakeholders to play particular roles on the project team throughout or at specific times in the project.

- Written documentation that captures roles and responsibilities of all stakeholders

- A Kickoff Meeting that orients all project team members to their roles and responsibilities and gets the project started (often supported by a Responsibility/Accountability Matrix)

3. Figure out exactly what the finished work products will be.

Results of Successful Performance:

- A series of conversations, brainstorming sessions, and other formal/ informal discussions about specific project deliverables

- A Work Breakdown Structure (WBS) in rough form as created by a brainstorming group (i.e., a bunch of yellow stickies spread out all over a wall, a collection of flip chart pages scribbled with items, a rough "mind map," etc.)

- A polished WBS which clearly lists 1) all interim deliverables that the end user will not see (such as scripts, flow charts, outlines, etc.) and 2) all finished deliverables that will be turned over to the user when the project is completed.

- A Project Scope Statement that expands the Project Charter to include the WBS and other items identified by the team in brainstorming sessions

- Approval of the Project Scope Statement and WBS by the sponsor and appropriate stakeholders.

4. Figure out what you need to do to complete the work products. (Identify tasks and phases.)

Results of Successful Performance:

- A list or graphical collection of all project tasks that must be completed to create project deliverables.

- A network diagram showing the sequence and flow of all project tasks, including opportunities for stakeholders to review and approve deliverables as they evolve

- Descriptions or illustrations of project phases

5. Estimate time, effort, and resources.

Results of Successful Performance:

- A detailed estimate of the duration, effort, and resources required to complete each project task

- A summary of duration, effort, and resources required for the entire project

6. Build a schedule.

Results of Successful Performance:

- One or more overview schedules showing the "big picture" of the project (i.e., showing all activities, phases, and major milestones). (Gantt, network diagram, summary table/calendar, etc.)

- One or more detailed schedules that expand or "zoom in" on particular parts of the overview schedule. (E.g., One particular project phase w/ detailed subtasks/tasks or one particular set of project players. (i.e., plumbers, computer programmers, senior executives w/approval points.)

- A strategy to revisit the schedule periodically in order to keep it up to date.

7. Estimate the costs.

Results of Successful Performance:

- An estimate of project costs, including the costs of labor, materials, supplies, and any other costs tracked by your organization, such as various overhead costs, etc.

- A description of all assumptions made in the cost estimate

8. Keep the project moving.

Results of Successful Performance:

- Periodic progress checks of each dimension of the project as spelled out in the project artifacts above (Charter, Effort/Duration table, Schedule, Cost Estimate, etc.)

- Project manager inspection and awareness of overall progress toward completion

- Project manager interventions to correct problems, remove obstacles, and keep the project moving as planned

9. Handle scope changes.

Results of Successful Performance:

- Adjustments to the project plan to deal with additions, reductions or modifications to the deliverables or work process

- Formal documentation of each scope change

- Formal approval of each scope change

10. Close out phases, close out the project.

Results of Successful Performance:

- Sponsor sign-off and approval of incrementally-evolving project deliverables and phases as they are completed

- Sponsor sign-off and approval of all finished project deliverables and the overall completed project

- Completion of typical project-specific follow-up activities (Project Archive, Post Mortem, Lessons Learned, hand-off/training, performance evaluations, etc.)

WORKING WITH YOUR TEAM AND MAINTAINING YOUR SANITY

This Part deals with some of the interpersonal "people stuff" that makes working with project teams so challenging. It includes "war stories" and specific strategies that might help the project manager and the team work together more effectively, get better results and feel good about participating on any project.

READY, FIRE, AIM? OR SEEK FIRST TO UNDERSTAND?

One of the things I most enjoy about teaching project management (PM) is the deeper knowledge of the field I get when students share their insights. A while back I asked my Franklin University PM students to write a brief essay answering this question: "Assume you are one of the guest authors for the e-book "One Simple Thing to Improve Projects or Project Management".....what would be your 'One Simple Thing?'"

Now this is one of my favorite questions to ask of everyone who's been involved in project work or PM. It triggers their "wisdom filters" as they sift through all the projects they've worked on (good and bad) to find that one simple thing. And best of all, it helps them clarify their own deeply held PM values. So it's always enlightening to hear what people come up with.

This time one of the students in the class included this in her essay (my bold added): "... The common issue among all the projects is that the **person in charge does not have one bit of understanding when it comes to the job and the job tasks.** This is because the boss **does not take the time to understand...**" Seeing this posted on the discussion board, another student responded with this: "...I'm always a 'worker bee'... so I am often frustrated when the **person dictating resource allocation and timeline does not understand the work** that must be done." Reacting to this comment, the first student elaborated with: "... **People really do not spend the time talking.** [We have] **a McDonald's drive-through mentality.** I think it is time we all learn to take a step back and talk about it before we move on to the next thing."

The Origins of "Ready, Fire, Aim" Decision Making

Now this interchange got me thinking about all the "Ready, Fire, Aim" decision making I've seen in my career. Overloaded with tasks and projects, project managers struggle to keep up with it all. And they inevitably cut corners — frequently satisfying themselves with a superficial awareness (as opposed to deeper, nuanced comprehension) of what those "worker bees" really do. It's unlikely that any project manager will take time to make that "deep dive" into the details of the work done by all the specialists on the team.

And beyond the sheer magnitude of the work load, there's the the problem of something that might be called **"focus interruptus."** I've written about this before in "Managing People with Self-Induced ADHD (er... Chronic Multitaskers)." This problem is pervasive and becoming worse every day. In her New York Times Book review of Douglas Rushkoff's new book Present Shock, Janet Maslin writes: **"... we are stuck with 'a diminishment of everything that isn't happening right now — and the onslaught of everything that supposedly is.' ...Your new boss isn't the person in the corner office; it's the P.D.A. in your pocket."**

For project managers, the net result of this fragmented consciousness is a choppy, incomplete awareness of reality that is simply an inadequate framework for good PM decision making. In this context, decisions are made based on hazy impressions and a jumble of random mental snapshots rather than a full, robust knowledge of job tasks, team roles, and subtle, work-related distinctions that would sharpen decision-making.

Your PM Challenge: Make the Time to Understand

In his classic *The Seven Habits of Highly Effective People*, Stephen Covey identifies Habit 5 as, "Seek first to understand, then to be understood."

In other words, Covey's effective people withhold judgment — withhold their decision-making — until they have a solid understanding of what the other person is all about. So **an effective project manager, in Covey's terms, would never put together a work plan or make work task-related decisions without a complete comprehension of the work itself and the people doing it.** (See my related blog post/audio podcast *Listen, Understand, Collaborate*.)

So how about it, project manager? Is it time you unplugged and locked yourself in a quiet room with your key team specialists to do that deep dive into what they really do for a living? ... to ask them which of your choices, large and small, are getting in the way of their effectiveness? **Is it time you shifted from "Ready, fire, aim!" to "Seek first to understand...?"**

BALANCING AUTHORITY AND RESPONSIBILITY: IT'S ALL ABOUT TRUST!

They gotta match!

Remember the first time you were trusted — truly trusted — to act on behalf of someone? Maybe it was babysitting your kid brother so your parents could have that special night out or taking care of your aunt's favorite plants and her beloved old dog while she went on vacation. You know the kind of trust I'm talking about: the kind that weighs on you a little and causes you to take a deep breath and say to yourself, "I can do this! This is really important and I can do this!" Remember what that felt like the first time you experienced it?

That kind of trust can be a powerful motivator. And it can be even more compelling when it's accompanied by the full authority – money, tools, decision-making power – to take action. Feeling the responsibility for handling an important job and knowing you have the authority to make things happen somehow helps you stand a little taller and strengthens your resolve to do great work — to prove that the trust isn't misplaced. So, in the end, trusting people completely can inspire them to do their best.

So You Say You Trust Me? Prove It!

To clarify, it's not enough for you to say, "I trust you to do this job" and then withhold meaningful authority by requiring me to ask your permission to make simple decisions or by forcing me to beg for resources to get the job done. No. **If you really trust me to do the job, then you'll give me the full authority (decision-making power, money, tools, people, etc.) that enables me to do it.** By granting me this breadth of authority, you **prove** that you trust me. And, given that proof, I will be more likely to work hard to ensure that your trust hasn't been misplaced.

This balance between authority and responsibility is an important component of all sorts of human relationships. When we strive for and maintain this balance, we ultimately prove that we respect the dignity of those whom we've tasked with doing a job. In ethical terms, **getting this balance right is simply the fair and decent thing to do!** Whether the work to be done is within the context of your family, a formal work team in an organization or society at large, it's critical to achieve. (Click here for a five-minute video that helps illustrate these concepts. You'll find it in my YouTube Playlist, Project Management [General Topics]: https://www.youtube.com/user/greerspm/playlists)

The questions below can help you make practical use of these ideas.

Reflections

Reflect on these questions:

- Are you conscious of the authority/responsibility balance when you assign work to team members?

- Do you have enough authority to do all the chores assigned to you? (If not, how might you get this authority?)

- What specific actions could you take on behalf of your project team or yourself to better balance the authority and responsibilities of everyone working on your projects?

Team Challenges

Ask your team:

- Do you feel adequately empowered to do the work assigned to you? (If not, what additional power or resources do you need?)

- Do you recall any specific situations in which you lacked adequate authority (resources or power) to do your job? (If so, what can we do to prevent this from happening again?)

Project Manager Challenges

- Make certain that everyone on your project team has the power to get and use all the resources they need to do their assigned tasks.

- Make certain that everyone on your project team has the power to make all the routine decisions necessary to keep from getting "stuck."

- Make sure you don't micromanage your team.

- If you are currently being micromanaged by your senior managers or don't have enough authority to make key decisions to keep your project moving or lack the resources (people, tools, money, etc.) to get good results, then resolve to do what you need to do (have that "tough talk" or confront that difficult senior manager) and get your authority and responsibility in balance!

ARE YOU CAUSING SUFFERING FOR YOUR PROJECT TEAM?

*(This book excerpt is from "Understand & Manage Your Stress" in **The Project Management Minimalist: Just Enough PM to Rock Your Projects!**)*

Best Practice: Consciously choose your attitude.

"We cannot choose our external circumstances, but we can always choose how we respond to them."
— Epictetus in **The Enchiridion**

*"From the most simple task to the most complex, **if you are not in a state of either acceptance, enjoyment, or enthusiasm, look closely and you will find that you are creating suffering for yourself and others.**"*
— Eckhart Tolle in **A New Earth**

Take another look at the Tolle quote above. The selection in bold tells the whole story. The graphic above illustrates how one man's thrashing against reality – his self-chosen misery – is creating suffering for himself and others!

So what should this guy be doing? Well, according to Tolle, **he only has three choices.**

1. He can **accept his situation** and stop wasting energy fighting against it. (This will allow him to think more clearly and figure out how to make things better.)
2. He can find something to **enjoy** about the situation.
3. He can become **enthusiastic** about the situation.

Any of these choices will make things better for himself and those around him.

Now when you think about it, he actually has **a fourth choice: He can remove himself from the situation by simply quitting his job.** That is, he can go somewhere else and do something else that won't make him so unhappy.

But if he can't quit or remove himself, then he must accept, enjoy, or become enthusiastic about his situation. To thrash around against reality, bemoaning the situation and spilling negative energy all over other people, is simply stupid. Worse, it saps away energy that could be used to make the changes that could improve things.

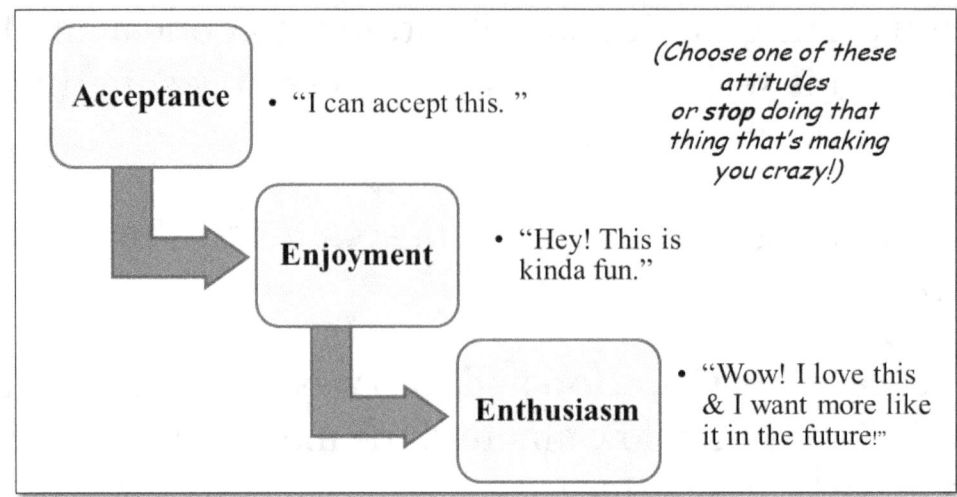

If you can't accept, enjoy or become enthusiastic, then stop doing it!

So the next time you find yourself ranting and raving and thrashing around against reality, refer to the chart above. See if you can't reduce your stress and make things better for everyone around you by consciously choosing a different attitude!

_____

Note: There's more about how you can "Consciously Choose Your Attitude," in the 3rd part of **The Project Management Minimalist: ... (The People Stuff))**. *You can also check out my 18-minute podcast, "Consciously Choose Your Attitude," here.*

NURTURING CORN STALKS AMONG THE SOYBEANS

A few years ago I was walking along the road near our summer home in Northwestern PA when I crested a hill and saw the scene pictured here. Now in case you don't have a farmer's crop-savvy eye, I'll tell you that this field was planted as a field of soybeans.* And soybeans in this part of the country don't typically grow above waist high.

Yet there they were. A few rowdy-looking corn plants popping up among all these otherwise sleepy-looking soybeans. Like giant exclamation points, these guys randomly punctuated what should have been a uniformly short collection of soy plants.

Since I sometimes wax philosophical on these walks, I was particularly receptive to the story they seemed to be telling me. The theme was simple. Dare to stand out. Dare to reach for the sky. Go ahead and be different, if you're feeling it. And most importantly, be true to yourself and don't be afraid to stand a little taller than everyone else. And as this theme crystallized in my mind, I found myself opening up to their energy.

I thought about how it must have been when they first poked their budding longish leaves above ground, surrounded and shaded by the chubby soy leaves. And I thought about how they somehow managed to catch enough sunlight to stir them to life... to encourage them to reach out and start their comparatively excessive journey toward the sky. And I wondered if the soy plants were a little surprised to see these ones-that-don't-belong-here rocketing up far above them just a few weeks after they invaded their otherwise all-soy spaces.

And then I began thinking about how new ideas are sometimes like these seemingly out-of-place, rowdy-looking corn plants. At first they just seem like some sort of weird accident. Something that will go away if we just ignore it. Then the existence of one stimulates another one, followed by the growth of still more. And the first thing you know, there are a whole bunch of voices supporting an idea that was entirely unexpected. And after all, aren't most creative breakthroughs, at first, unexpected surprises?

All things considered, I decided that there was something beautiful and inspiring about these gangly, out-of-place, wildly sturdy plants that managed to thrive despite their surroundings. And **I resolved that I would be on the lookout for gangly, out-of-place ideas on my project teams. And when I find such ideas I'll be careful not to fear them as freakish invaders, but instead nurture them to see what surprises and creative leaps they may have in store for us.**

---

* Want to see more pictures of soybeans? C'mon... you know you do! If you eat soy products, you should pay your respects to the amazing plant that produces the beans! See my Google Plus album, **Soybeans [Yep, Soybeans!** (Go to https://plus.google.com/photos/+MichaelGreer/albums/5662785521508148193)

MANAGING PEOPLE WITH SELF-INDUCED ADHD (ER... CHRONIC MULTITASKERS)

"... multitasking people not only perform each task less suitably, but lose time in the process."

You see it all the time. Wherever a group of people gathers, someone sits with hands cupped around a small object held at about knee level, thumbs flying as he dispenses text characters to a far off receiver. Every few seconds he glances up to make quick, token eye contact with the person speaking, not really seeing the speaker, but offering up a glassy-eyed stare or vacant smile while his brain contemplates the content of the pixels on his screen. Sometimes he hazards a not-always-appropriate comment, then it's quickly back to his little LCD screen. At other times, you think you're engaged in a task-focused, one-on-one conversation when suddenly the table vibrates or a ring tone chirps and the person you're talking to is gone, staring at the screen and clicking away a response to a distant contact who simply couldn't wait for a reply.

Meanwhile, somewhere down the hall, hidden away from prying eyes, a writer lurches along forming a sentence, beginning another, then being jolted out of her flow by a little beep announcing the arrival of a new chat message or a fresh news headline. Whether this latest incoming information is of value to the writer's project really doesn't matter. It immediately gets full mindshare and pulls attention away from the moment. And when the writer returns to the piece she was creating, she struggles for a few minutes getting back into the rhythms of her phrasing.

They Call It Multitasking

They call it multitasking. And those who practice it are sometimes smugly proud of their ability to do it. But here's what Wikipedia tells us about multitasking (my bold added):

"Since the 1990s, experimental psychologists have started experiments on the nature and limits of human multitasking. It has been shown multitasking is not as workable as concentrated times. In general, these **studies have disclosed that people show severe interference when even very simple tasks are performed at the same time**, if both tasks require selecting and producing action... Many researchers believe that action planning represents a 'bottleneck' in which the human brain can only perform one task at a time. **Psychiatrist Richard Hallowell has gone so far as to describe multitasking as a 'mythical activity** in which people believe they can perform two or more tasks simultaneously.' ...

Because the brain cannot fully focus when multitasking, people take longer to complete tasks and are predisposed to error. **When people attempt to complete many tasks at one time, or [alternate] rapidly between them, errors go way up and it takes far longer — often double the time or more — to get the jobs done than if they were done sequentially...** This is largely because the brain is compelled to restart and refocus... [One study] found that in the interim between each exchange, the brain makes no progress whatsoever. Therefore, multitasking people not only perform each task less suitably, but lose time in the process." — http://en.wikipedia.org/wiki/Human_multitasking

I Call It Self-Induced ADHD

ADHD is defined as "attention deficit hyperactivity disorder." Wikipedia tells us that: "Inattention, hyperactivity, and impulsivity are the key behaviors of ADHD." The article goes on to list **these symptoms** (among many others) **exhibited by people who have ADHD:**

- ... easily distracted, miss details, forget things, and frequently switch from one activity to another

- ... difficulty focusing on one thing

- Become bored with a task after only a few minutes, unless they are doing something enjoyable

- ... difficulty focusing attention on organizing and completing a task or learning something new

- ... trouble completing or turning in ... assignments, often losing things (e.g., pencils, toys, assignments) needed to complete tasks or activities

- ... Not seem to listen when spoken to..." — http://en.wikipedia.org/wiki/Attention-deficit_hyperactivity_disorder

In my view, the symptoms above describe many of the self-labeled "multitaskers" who show up in my classes, in meetings, and in social settings ranging from having lunch to enjoying a holiday get-together. And, despite their protests to the contrary, in work-related settings they are simply not as effective as they believe themselves to be. Consider this from, Deborah Gray, a writer who has ADHD and enjoys multitasking (my bold added):

"**According to a study at Stanford University, I'm probably not as effective at multi-tasking as I think I am.** Researchers put both a group of habitual heavy multi-taskers, people who frequently are receiving multiple streams of unrelated input at one time, and a group of light multi-taskers through a series of three tests to find out how effective they actually were. They hoped to find that the heavy multi-taskers had some kind of natural ability that allowed them to divide their attention effectively.

What they found, instead, was that the **heavy multi-taskers were worse at multi-tasking than the light multi-taskers.** So what accounts for this perception that heavy multi-taskers can have that they're more effective when multi-tasking? One of the study authors theorized in an interview on NPR's Science Friday that frequent multi-taskers just enjoy doing things that way." – Deborah Gray, "Are We Good at Multi-Tasking?" — http://www.healthcentral.com/adhd/c/8689/105759/good-multi-tasking

Helping Compulsive Multitaskers Become More Effective

From the perspective of a project manager who is trying to keep people focused on project results, **there seems to be no practical reason to distinguish compulsive multitaskers from those who suffer from ADHD.** Therefore, if we want to help these people become more effective on our projects, we need to be aware of some of the tips and tools that ADHD treatment professionals suggest for their patients. The website

ADHDActionGuide.com provides personalized suggestions for coping with ADHD based on your taking a short assessment. I believe **many of these tips could help our compulsive multitaskers (those with self-induced ADHD) become more effective on our project teams.** Here's a list of some that seem most promising:

Some "Tips for Work" from ADHDActionGuide.com

- Don't let yourself be interrupted. At work, **commit to time blocks when you'll let the phone and e-mail go unanswered while you focus on the task at hand.** If you work in an office, don't allow colleagues to drop in and take you off track. Instead, suggest that they make appointments to meet with you.

- Control interruptions, **don't let interruptions control you.** Don't get caught up in another situation until you've completed what you're currently doing.

- While at your desk, **keep only what you're working on in front of you.** Get everything else out of your line of sight.

- As someone is talking to you, check in periodically to what's being said. **Paraphrasing is a good way to make sure you understand.**

- When working, especially **when doing challenging work, find quiet times when others are not around**; close your door for added privacy, come in early, work when others take lunch, etc.

- See if your **desk can be placed in an area free from distractions,** such as windows and doors, preferably in an area with less traffic. It'll keep your mind from wandering and discourage unexpected visitors.

- Have an office? **Arrange furniture so your desk faces away from the doorway.** It discourages people from walking in and interrupting you.

- **When someone makes a request, repeat it aloud** so you hear yourself saying it. This also helps ensure that you both heard the request accurately.

- **Use a color code system** of file folders at your desk to keep track of deadlines, due dates, birthdays, school or child information, and tasks to be completed.

- Divide tasks according to your strengths. **Doing things you are best at first will help increase your chances of sticking to them** through completion. This may help you finish unwanted chores as well.

- **Use a printed or electronic day planner.** Write in daily appointments, important dates to remember, and time allotted for important tasks to be completed. Be sure to include personal things you want to get done as well, like working out, kids' activities, etc.

- **Don't critique what you're doing until you've completed it.** That way, you can avoid getting distracted by perfectionism or frustrated at how much you have left to do.

Some "Tips for the Home" from ADHDActionGuide.com

[PM translation: Tips for enhancing interpersonal skills?]

- **Face people and make eye contact when speaking with them.** It lets them know you're paying attention and helps you do exactly that.

- **Pause after expressing each point in a conversation**, and wait for a response before continuing to talk.

- **When someone's speaking, concentrate on waiting until he/she ends his/her sentence** before you jump in. If you have a question, ask permission before asking it: "Excuse me, may I ask a question?"

- **Listening silently** to someone's long story bonds them socially to you. And all you have to do is be silent!

- If you impulsively blurt out comments that you later regret, **learn to take notes, and write down what you're thinking of saying.** This will give you time to consider: Is this a good thing to say? What is the best way to say it?

- **Slow down. A breath between sentences** will help you control the rush of words bursting out of your mouth and give others a chance to take in what you have to say.

I recommend you share the lists above with your project team.

Better yet, have the appropriate members of your team go to the ADHDActionGuide.com website and take the personalized assessment, followed by the

> *There seems to be no practical reason to distinguish compulsive multitaskers from those who suffer from ADHD...*

personalized diagnosis and suggestions. Talk about this together as a team or in one-on-one sessions with your worst offenders. This way you can get a helpful dialogue started about all your team's multitaskers and how you can increase their effectiveness.

Conclusion: Don't Try to Work Stoned!

Here's a pertinent quote from Brian Johnson's PhilosophersNotes on Tal Ben-Shahar's book *Happier: Learn the Secrets to Daily Joy and Lasting Fulfillment.* Brian writes:

"For the record, when Ben-Shahar tells us that 'checking our e-mail every few minutes takes away from our productivity and creativity and ultimately makes us less happy,' he's not making a flippant remark. He cites a study that shows workers so distracted suffer a greater loss of IQ than someone smoking marijuana."

So... **would you tolerate your project team members lowering their IQ by smoking marijuana on the job? Probably not. Then how can**

you ignore the potential loss of effectiveness that comes from their twitchy multi-tasking or "self-induced ADHD?" As project manager, you need to help your compulsive multitaskers find ways to unplug from the data stream, focus on handling one task at a time, and increase the quality of their work.

As Brian Tracy says in his book *Focul Point*:

"When you concentrate single-mindedly on a single task, without diversion or distraction, you get it done far faster than if you start and stop and then come back to the task and pick it up again. You can reduce the amount of time you spend on a major task by as much as 80 percent simply by refusing to do anything else until that task is complete."

So for the sake of your project's efficiency, and the sanity of your project team, **you have an obligation to help your compulsive multitaskers kick the habit** and transcend their self-induced ADHD!

REFLECTIONS ON SOCHI, THE "SECOND SCREEN" AND HALF-BAKED DECISIONS

(Is anyone listening? ... Anyone at all??)

A while back I tried to watch the Opening Ceremony of the Winter Olympics in Sochi. I say **tried** because I eventually became so frustrated by Matt Lauer's and Meredith Vieira's endless stream of intrusive babble that I switched the whole thing off. From what I saw, the ceremony had been painstakingly designed by its Olympic hosts to tell a story. The producers of the event had obviously worked hard to weave together a collection of objects, images, performers and music to create a spectacular narrative that highlighted Russia's history.

Was it mere propaganda? Was it an idealized rewriting of history? Frankly, I can't say because every time I started to become absorbed by the narrative and allow its images and music to carry me along with it, Lauer or Vieira would yank me out of the story line with their own narrative. And since theirs consisted mostly of arcane trivia, details of the mechanics of the production, or political editorializing, I found it impossible to sustain the sense of wonder that the grand production had been designed to stimulate. Unfortunately, turning off the sound to shut off their prattling also muted the beautiful music and sound effects. So I finally just gave up in disgust and switched the whole thing off.

A Colossal Waste!

As the room became silent, I found myself wondering about — and feeling sympathy for — the producers of the event. They clearly had undertaken months of preparation. They constructed a logical "through line" that told their story, then they rehearsed and coordinated hundreds of moving parts. In short, **they had attempted to deliver a powerfully moving and cohesive viewer experience. Yet here sat these American TV talking heads intruding themselves at random throughout the event, dragging viewers on endless, mood-destroying side trips** and distracting us from absorbing any coherent message or from being swept away in the spectacle. What a colossal waste!

Like Your Last Business Presentation?

The more I thought about it, however, the more I realized that **this NBC-broadcast of the Sochi Olympic Opening Ceremony was an apt metaphor for many business meetings I've attended**. The same elements are present:

- Someone works hard to prepare a logical narrative, often supported with multi-media components.

- This person rehearses, then delivers the presentation.

- Members of the audience ostensibly attend to the presentation.

- Members of the audience are ceaselessly, often pointlessly, interrupted by their own, personal talking heads in the form of the ever-present "second screen" of a smartphone or tablet.

- These interrupted members of the audience, in turn, become someone else's "second screen" interruptions as their fingers tap out terse little messages that intrude into another presenter's carefully-crafted presentation.

The result of all this fracturing of a presenter's logical, cohesive message is that attendees acquire an understanding of it that is incomplete or badly distorted.

Half-Baked Comprehension = Half-Baked Decisions!

Now here's the big deal: What distinguishes these business presentations from the Olympics Opening Ceremony is that **those attending are frequently called upon to take an action or make a decision at the conclusion. But if your recall of the presenter's message is sketchy or skewed, your comprehension is… well… half-baked! And half-baked comprehension can only lead to half-baked decisions!**

So here's **your challenge:** The next time you attend a meeting, try to fully "attend" to the presentation. Put yourself in the shoes of the presenter. Try to imagine the effort she expended to accumulate information, sift it down to its essences and build a presentation that would be engaging and informative. Then ask yourself if it makes good business sense to allow your own jabbering little device (your pocket-sized network talking head) to ceaselessly interrupt and water down your engagement.

FORGIVE THEM. IT'S JUST THEIR INNER CHIHUAHUA.

The other morning I stepped out of my quiet meditation space and into the kitchen for breakfast. I knew that storms had been ravaging some parts of the country where I have relatives, so I decided that instead of the usual quick weather check on the net, I'd turn on the TV to get a national perspective and maybe see some regional video.

As the TV screen popped on, I was immediately jolted by a couple of those angry talking heads. These guys were debating the merits of a recent supreme court decision. I had my hands busy with food prep, so instead of clicking away, I endured the rants and raves and posturing and dire predictions of social implosion that these two "opponents" predicted would surely flow from either adopting or failing to adopt this decision as the law of the land. Clearly their intent was to inflame the passions of their respective constituencies, one ultra conservative & the other strongly liberal (progressive).

Now what struck me about all this was the purely speculative nature of all the arguments. Each drew upon the fears of his particular group of regular fans. And each hyperbolically predicted extreme, even outrageous, consequences that were designed to stimulate a strong visceral response to some imagined (but by no means certain) future.

This sort of "discussion" is the political equivalent of the noises exuded by a side show barker: It is cheap, sensational, and often distorted.

The Invisible Background Hum of Anger

Unfortunately, this kind of stuff makes up a substantial portion of every news channel's programming. **The result is that vast numbers of people go around vaguely angry at talking-head conjured demons, real or imagined, who threaten their lives. With this steady stream of venom radiating through the airwaves, many of us live with a pervasive hum of background anger churning away, just below our conscious awareness.** As we move through the day encountering people, we don't see them as the unique individuals they are. Instead we see archetypes who are for or against abortion, gun rights, the social safety net, big government, gay marriage and on and on. Worse, we see them as threats to be feared.

If you think you're immune to this, you need only spend time in daily mindful meditation. You may be surprised to find how much of this crap bubbles up!

Aarrgghh!! Make It Stop!

So how can we get rid of these angry thoughts and background anger? The short answer, of course, is to stop listening to these media performers – – just turn them off. But that leaves us with all the negative seeds they've already planted. What do we do about the residual anger these inevitably sprout?

Like any malady, it must be witnessed and accepted before it can be dealt with. **You gotta call it what it really is: fear.** As Alan Cohen tells us (my bold added):

"**Anger is fear under pressure.** Behind every angry upset there is a fear. If you attempt to deal with anger at the level of anger alone – by either venting it or repressing it – you are manipulating the symptom without addressing the cause. If you can discover the fear behind the anger and dismantle it in the light of awareness, the anger dissipates. The next time you are angry, ask yourself, What am I afraid of?" — from *A Daily Dose of Sanity: A Five-Minute Soul Recharge for Every Day of the Year* by Alan Cohen via Brian Johnson's PhilosophersNotes

In other words, **when fear gets a glimpse of itself it often begins blustering and posturing to hide its true nature.** In an effort to maintain its dignity, fear morphs into quasi-ferocious anger. **Like a chihuahua about to be sniffed by a Great Dane, fear barks and growls and desperately bares its teeth to ward off an imagined disaster.** Never mind that the Great Dane was simply curious. It's driven away before any kind of mutual understanding can be reached. And sadly, both end the encounter as ignorant of each other as they began it.

Still, there are exceptions. We've all seen those heart-warming examples of big, scary creatures hanging out with — even nuzzling and playing with — frail little creatures. So how can this happen?

The answer is first-hand experience. Familiarity. A one-to-one connection that allows each to find something good... even enjoyable... in the other. When this happens, fear melts away and the veil of anger disappears.

The Old Man and the Sea

Here's a human example. I once knew an old fellow who had fought in World War II. He didn't hesitate to tell scary tales of what "those damned Japs" did to U.S. soldiers. This was usually followed by loud and long and politically incorrect rants against the success of Japanese cars, electronics products, etc. in today's U.S. marketplace. The thing is, since he had lived most of his life in rural Appalachia, he had never actually met a Japanese person.

One day, during one of his a rare visits to our home in Los Angeles, I took this old curmudgeon ocean fishing. It was his first such excursion and he was uncharacteristically enthusiastic about the adventure. In the pre-dawn darkness we boarded one of those big, tugboat-sized boats that made daily runs a mile or two out into Santa Monica Bay in search of bass, rock cod, and other sport fish. There were about 25 of us on deck, bundled in light jackets and hooded sweatshirts to ward off the chill of the sea breeze and fog.

When the sun finally rose and burned off that morning fog, we were miles out to sea, the dock no longer anywhere in sight. What was in sight, however, were the faces of our fellow fishermen. They were Black and Hispanic and Asian and Anglo and several other subtly blended races that make up our richly multi-ethnic Southern California. Looking around and realizing who his traveling companions were, Old Dude wrinkled his brow, raised his eyebrows, and shot me some question marks. I silently returned a nod and a reassuring smile, then struck up a conversation with a couple of our comrades. Soon the interpersonal ice was broken and everyone began swapping their favorite fish-catching strategies.

As the day wore on, Old Dude joined in. And to my surprise, he bonded with an old Japanese-American fellow about his age. A couple of hours into the trip, they were taking turns watching each other's poles while one of them would take a bathroom break, get a coffee, or go after more bait. By the end of the trip they were trading stories about kids, grandkids, and other details of their lives. In short, they had become friends. On the drive home he summed up his feelings for this man:

"Helluva nice fella! And he knows a lot about deep sea fishin'!" Through first-hand experience and the magic of one-on-one contact, old Dude's fear-based anger at Japanese in the abstract had melted away, replaced by the reality of his new friend's humanity.

A Toothy Growl Means a Nervous Chihuahua

So the next time you find yourself working with someone who's suffering from media-induced anger toward a group of people who differ in their politics, religion, sexual orientation, etc., ask yourself: "Does this angry person actually know any real, living examples of this group? Have they talked to them and tried to understand what animates their choices. Or tried to learn who they are as individuals?" If the answer is "No," then it may make sense to simply ignore their anger.

But if their anger persists, you might want to ask them an important question, namely, "What, exactly, are you afraid of?" If they answer you honestly, then you may begin to see their anger for what it truly is: Nothing more than their inner chihuahua twitching nervously and barking out of ignorance! And this nervous little critter quite likely deserves your compassion.

---

* Chihuahua image above from the YouTube video "Angry Chihuahua." Check it out! — http://www.youtube.com/watch?v=AKGPvul8FXc.

WHY IT'S POINTLESS TO ARGUE ABOUT POLITICS OR RELIGION

"There is nothing either good or bad, but thinking makes it so."
— from Shakespeare's Hamlet, Act II, scene ii

Everyone's heard this bit of advice: "Don't talk politics or religion with family and friends. It only causes arguments and hard feelings." What's more, most of us know that these topics should absolutely be avoided in business settings. After all, project teams have enough trouble meeting deadlines and keeping the peace among stakeholders. Why borrow trouble by getting into arguments about politics or religion? Still... When long hours keep your team together late at night and everyone begins to grow tired and grumpy or when you're relaxing together after hours at the coffee shop or tavern, it can happen. Someone let's slip a little political rant, a philosophical criticism, or a bit of religious dogma and wham! You're embroiled in one of these impossible-to-win battles.

Now, I'm a writer and a trainer. I like explaining things. And, unfortunately for my family and friends, I sometimes slip into my own passionate rants and extended speeches in support of my political or quasi-religious perspectives – "explaining" the seemingly unexplainable. Not surprisingly, this kind of behavior often produces a strong response from my listener, who soon begins his or her own passionate rant. These interchanges usually end as they do for anyone who indulges in such speechifying: In a total stalemate with my philosophical opponent or, worse, in silent frustration for each of us.

Later, after what could have been a pleasant conversation is long over, I find myself regretting the whole nasty interchange and wondering what happened. How could I, who can be so supportive and tolerant in the classroom or with my clients, manage to get into such ego-driven, horn-locking, polarizing disputes over these topics? After wrestling with this question for some time, I think I've finally figured out how these over-heated disputes happen. And I've also figured out why such disagreements are almost impossible to resolve.

It's All Personal... Really Personal!

Potential life-changing experiences

The cloud in the graphic shows a bunch of potentially powerful, life-changing events, experiences, or relationships that might float around in your consciousness. (Sure, you could add lots more items, but for the sake of this article, let's just pretend that those shown here are comprehensive.)

As we wander through life, we find ourselves idiosyncratically choosing all sorts of experiences based on the advice of parents, teachers, or friends. And sometimes it's not a matter of choice at all, but mere circumstance.

The world simply takes us places we never planned to go and delivers its lessons to us whether we seek them out or not.

Consider the stories of Mr. Green and Ms. Red.

What Mr. Green experienced

An Example: Mr. Green's Story

The cloud on the left shows Mr. Green's most significant life-changing experiences. Each is circled in green and together they tell the unique tale of his evolution. As a child, he read a powerful work of fiction whose protagonist completely captured his imagination. This character and his values became a filter through which Mr. Green viewed the world the rest of his life. Later, as a teen, he suffered through a bad relationship with his father, who drank heavily and often delivered verbal brow-beatings that left him emotionally scarred. This led Mr. Green to become severely intolerant of anyone who uses alcohol, no matter how responsibly they do so. In his early twenties, he travelled extensively throughout the South Pacific where exposure to the philosophies of several island cultures changed his views about the way a good society should operate. Early in his adult life he married his high-school sweetheart, only to find that over the years, as they matured, they grew apart and he ultimately endured a painful divorce. This left him questioning the role of marriage in society, as well as unable to trust that anyone could ever truly love or be loved.

Bullied in his middle-school years, he developed a "strike first" attitude about dealing with anybody who might show the least signs of aggression. And in college, after acquiring the mentorship of a college instructor whom he believed to be a truly brilliant leader in his field, he was deeply disappointed to learn that this person was a mere academic poser, focused on winning any political games necessary to obtain tenure and a life-long position at the university.

Another Example: Ms. Red's Story

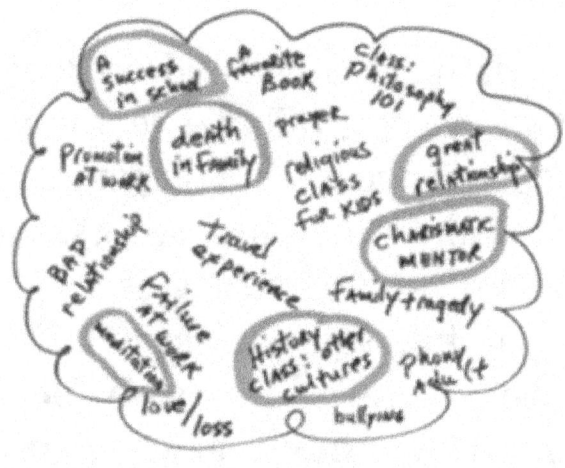

What Ms. Red experienced

In contrast, Ms. Red's cloud shows a life shaped by different, but equally powerful, experiences. Her early success as a winner of an elementary school science competition led her to a career in astrophysics, which molded both her religious perspectives and her attitude about the role of government in supporting the sciences and supporting humanity's quest to understand the cosmos. The death of her father, whom she loved dearly, strengthened her resolve to become politically active to help bring about his dream of a stronger science program in the public schools. Support from a charismatic and well-travelled mentor (whom she met in a comparative world culture class in college) helped her to make many connections within the international astrophysics community. This led to her aggressively acting as a champion of world-wide cooperation among scientists, sometimes placing her in opposition to national government leaders.

Discovering the power of meditation on one of her trips abroad, she now meditates regularly to help deal with stress and maintain her focus. Overall, she draws courage and energy from the many positive experiences that have shaped her as she pushes the boundaries of international scientific cooperation

Completely Different World Views

When their lives began, both Mr. Green and Ms. Red had a nearly infinite range of potential experiences available to them. Yet, through their idiosyncratic, unique experiences, life led them to completely different perspectives on political and religious matters. Each has developed a world view based on hard-fought struggles to derive meaning from powerful, sometimes painful, sometimes joyful, events they've lived through. And **these world views, precisely because they were so hard-fought, are something they feel they have earned and will continue to cling to as they refine their unique religious and political frameworks.**

So **when you tangle with either of them while arguing a particular** religious or political point, you are essentially tangling with all that history, all that pain, all those joys, and all those hard-fought struggles to find meaning.

Is it any wonder that in the midst of such arguments, when you find yourself blasted by a passionate roar from your opponent, you sometimes feel surprised and shocked? And you end up asking yourself: "Whoa! Where did that come from?"

The truth is, it's almost impossible for you to know fully "where it came from," since the passionate roar that you provoked has roots that go deep into this person's personal (and largely idiosyncratic) history.

Evolution of Personal Political & Religious Views: The Happy Face Version

So what might we generalize from the examples of Mr. Green and Ms. Red? The slightly whimsical graphic below summarizes what might be a reasonable model for the evolution of our religious and political beliefs.

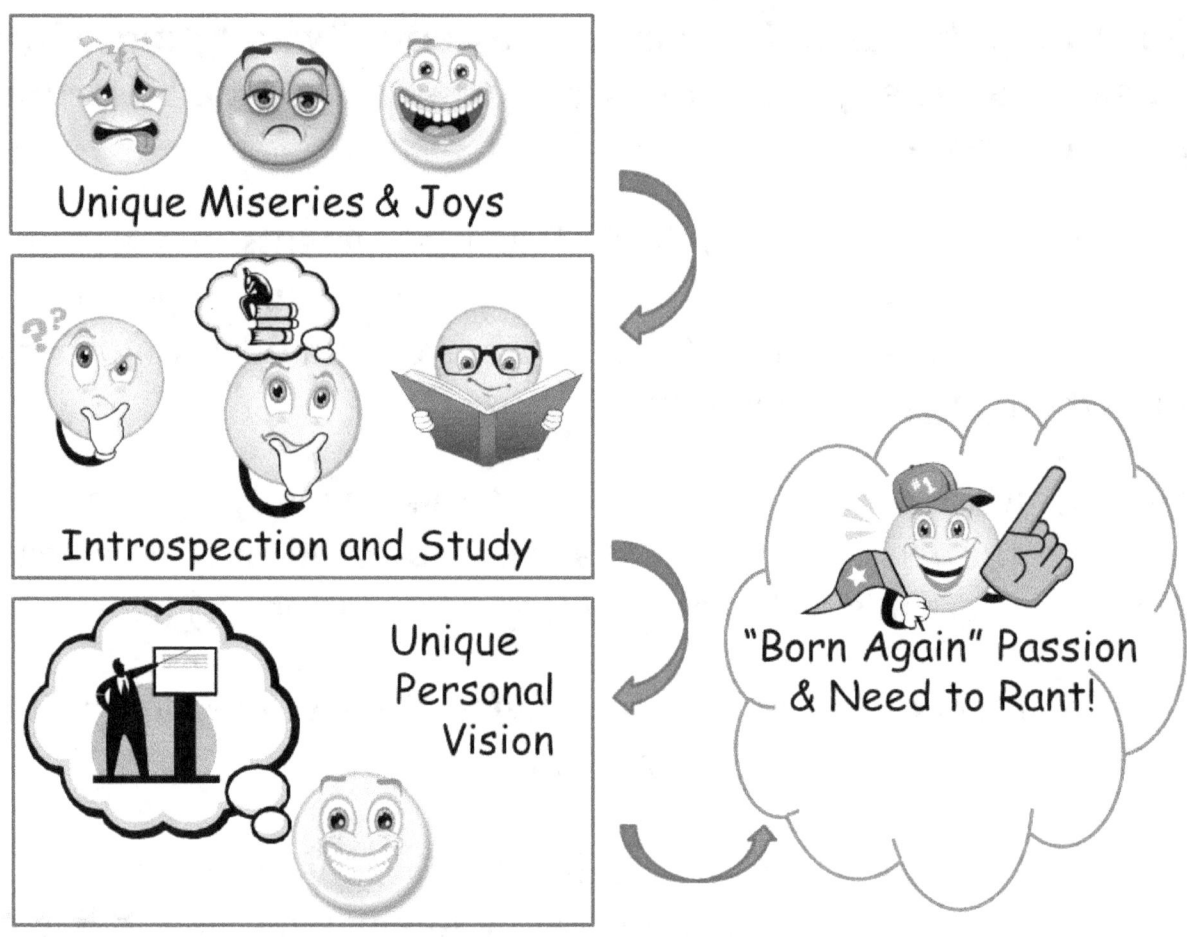

How our beliefs evolve: The Happy Face Model

In a nutshell, the unique miseries and joys we experience are powerful emotional events that take their toll and demand to be resolved. As these powerful emotional events pile up, we eventually develop an enormous need to become introspective as we try to figure out what they all mean. Sometimes this introspection prompts us to do relevant research. Often, however, the topics we are drawn to investigate usually resonate to the same emotional frequencies as the events that prompted our introspection. In other words, the topics of study that we seek out typically help us validate our experiences and help us decode the meaning in ways that seem consistent with our unique "cloud" of experiences.

Ultimately, we develop a distinctive personal vision of the way the world works. And given enough time to fall in love with it, we might even develop our own "born again" passion for this vision and set forth to preach our newly discovered gospel to anyone who'll listen. We don't necessarily mean any harm or disrespect with such preaching... we just want to share that amazing, empowering feeling that washed over us when we finally "figured it all out!"

Evolution of Personal Religious & Political Views: The Waterfall Version

Now if you are a student of project management or if you dislike happy faces, you might find the diagram below to be more palatable than the previous — especially since it looks more "serious," and resembles the structures often used to depict project life cycles.

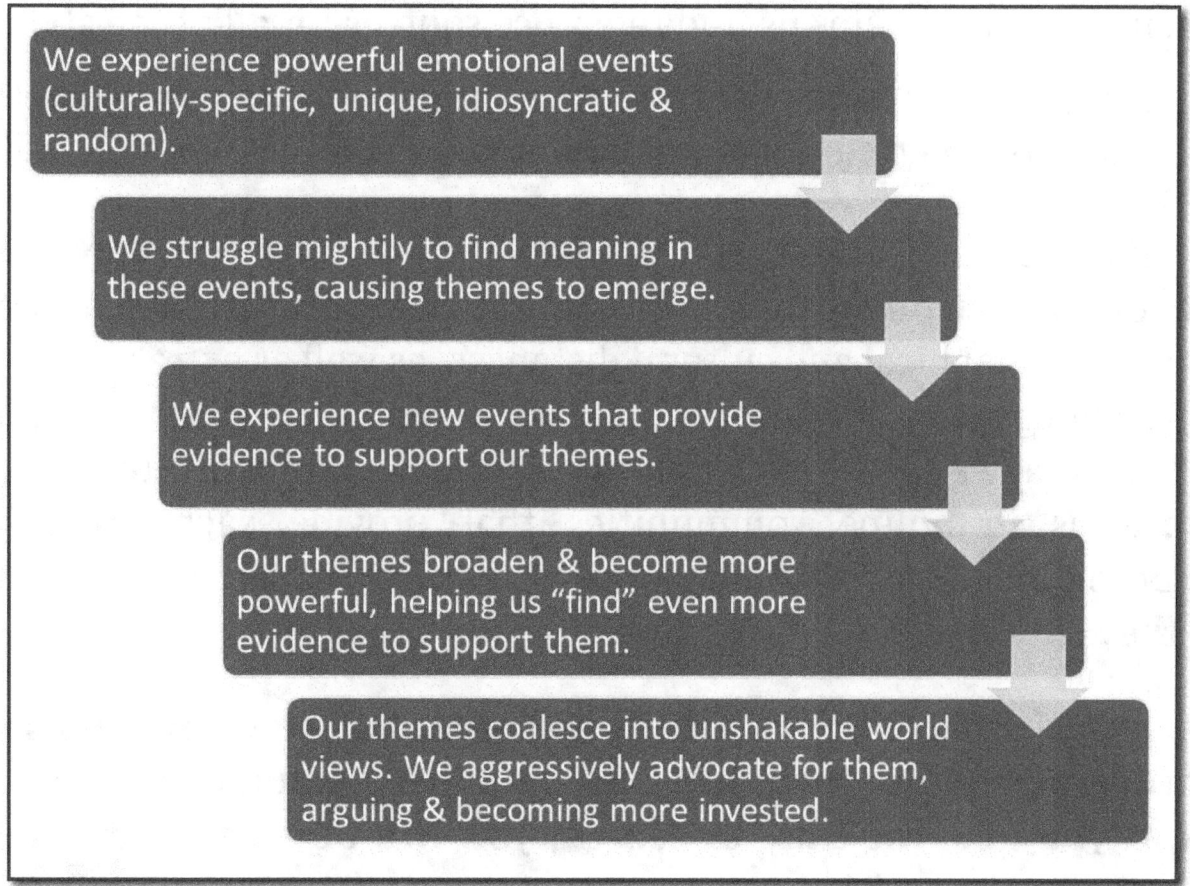

We experience powerful emotional events (culturally-specific, unique, idiosyncratic & random).

We struggle mightily to find meaning in these events, causing themes to emerge.

We experience new events that provide evidence to support our themes.

Our themes broaden & become more powerful, helping us "find" even more evidence to support them.

Our themes coalesce into unshakable world views. We aggressively advocate for them, arguing & becoming more invested.

How our beliefs evolve: The Waterfall Model.

The boxes speak for themselves. However, **there is this fairly daunting fact to consider: In each domain of thought, politics or religion, there is a nearly infinite collection of bits of evidence that can be found to support... and firmly cement in place... almost any chosen theme!**

In other words, **if you wish to cobble together a collection of "facts" to support a particular religious view or political philosophy we have plenty of sources** to draw upon, including:

- Thousands of years of recorded human history
- Thousands of human cultures with differing perspectives
- Thousands of authors and sacred texts, past and present
- An internet that helps us find reference sources for all of the above
- A daily stream of current events and editorial opinions served up by the internet and traditional media sources

The internet is particularly problematic because it allows easy collaboration among people who would otherwise be separated by extreme geographical and cultural distances, as well as extreme political and religious views. To put it a bit starkly, the 'net allows a handful of far-flung crazies who would otherwise have no real voice to assemble themselves in online communities that provide each other with substantial comfort and reinforcement for their ideas, no matter how odd they may seem to the rest of us!

My point: **No matter what political or religious viewpoint you select in order to breathe meaning into your life's unique miseries and joys, if you take the time to search, you will be able to find ample evidence to support it.**

Why It's Pointless to Argue About Politics or Religion

When clouds collide...

Now **here's the problem:** Most of the time our hard-won vision of how the world works remains quietly concealed in our hearts. Yet it's always there, just below the surface, waiting to explode all over anyone foolish enough to challenge us with a severely contradictory vision. After all, we've got way too much effort invested in this world view to allow it to be quickly changed by anyone. The result: Whether we like it or not, we sometimes stumble into one of those intense and unwinnable verbal battles we all find so frustrating.

Think about it: How can we ever know enough about the experiences and struggles-for-truth that lay beneath another person's world view to enable us to adequately judge its validity? **Can we really presume to be able to stand back and critique a world view that is built on a foundation of countless unique, idiosyncratic pains and joys that we ourselves have never experienced? Certainly not!** That's why if we try making such judgments, we soon learn that the emotional energy behind our listener's world view generates a vigorous argument that ultimately leads nowhere... aside from an exchange of philosophical generalities supported by carefully-chosen (and highly idiosyncratic and personal) anecdotes.

The bottom line: It's a waste of time (and toxic to your relationships) to indulge in arguments over religious or political philosophies.

So Don't Argue: Be an Anthropologist... And Try to See Into the Cloud

In matters of political or religious opinion, as Star Trek's Borg might say: "Resistance is futile!" **One well-intentioned passionate assertion bangs against another well-intentioned passionate assertion. Or one negative rant is met by an opposing negative rant.** Either way, smacking together all these visions and theories and end-point conclusions and derived meanings is simply futile. When you are confronted with a broad philosophical conclusion without "seeing the work" of the person who solved the puzzle beneath it, it simply hangs in the air between you – where it is met by your own alternative broad philosophical conclusion. The result: At best, you'll be talking past each other. At worst, you become disrespected for the "stupidity" of your "ridiculous" position or make an enemy of your fellow debater.

Instead of getting ensnarled in one of these pointless interchanges, I recommend that you try to see into the cloud. That is, try to actively imagine the cloud of experiences that your fellow debater has experienced. Try to discern exactly his or her unique pains and joys. When you hear a political or religious or political assertion that starts to make you crazy, **try saying something like this:**

"Wow! That's interesting! How'd you come to that conclusion? Tell me more about what led you to this perspective."

Then, when your fellow philosopher begins to answer this question, **listen. Really listen. Listen with your heart. Try to see the links between her personal experiences and her formal philosophy.**

Become an amateur anthropologist, seeking to learn exactly what dwells inside that unique cloud of experience that has formed this person's world view. Listen to the position, accept it (not necessarily agree, simply accept it) as it stands. Ask where it came from, then listen, learn, ask for elaboration, probe, relate, empathize, and try your hardest to understand with both your head and your heart.

As Stephen Covey says, **"Seek first to understand than to be understood...** The deepest hunger of the human heart is to be understood, for understanding implicitly affirms, validates, recognizes and appreciates the intrinsic worth of another."

So instead of engaging in a political or religious battle, give someone the opportunity to be understood. Who knows? You may broaden your own perspective. And, better yet, maybe someday she'll return the favor.

Reflections

Reflect on these questions:

- Which of your project team member or project stakeholders seem to have political or religious perspectives that "make you crazy?"

- What, specifically, could you do to learn more about this person's evolution and how these perspectives were shaped?

- Despite your disagreements, what political or religious values might you have in common with this person?

Team Challenges

Ask your team (cautiously, tactfully, and only if it's OK in your organization's culture):

- Are there subtle ways that clashes in political or religious perspectives are getting in the way of our work?

- Could we try to be more sensitive to the unique personal history of our fellow team members or stakeholders in order to develop greater respect for their "different" world view?

Project Manager Challenges

Ask your team (again, cautiously, tactfully, & only if it's OK in your local culture.)

- If you observe serious clashes in political or religious perspectives between team members, encourage those who are clashing to "take a break," step back from their arguments, and share a little about their history and evolution. (Encourage each to listen, not judge, and learn about the other's life-shaping events and how these create a framework for their world-view.)

- Share this blog post, including the graphics, with those who are having philosophical clashes. Ask them to compare "clouds," share life-shaping experiences, and try to deeply understand (but not necessarily agree with) each other's world views.

THREE BROAD STRATEGIES TO REWARD AND MOTIVATE VOLUNTEERS ON YOUR PROJECT TEAM

These days most organizations are operating with the smallest possible number of employees. This means that project managers routinely find themselves having to reach beyond their organization's "official" employee roster to find team members. And frequently this means acquiring volunteers — team members who can't be paid or given any tangible compensation for their efforts. But **if you can't pay them or provide any material compensation, how can you reward volunteers for their work?** And, more importantly, how can you keep them motivated to do a good job and to join your project team the next time you need them?

Below are three broad strategies for rewarding and motivating volunteers.

1. Respect them and demonstrate your respect through your actions.

Specifically you can:

- **Take the time to understand their unique talents and skills**, then work with them to co-create unique roles for them on the project.

- **Ask for their help**, or at minimum their approval, **in defining their assigned tasks**, deadlines, review/approval points, etc.

- On their behalf, **fight for the time and resources** (tools, equipment, support staff, etc.) they will need so they can do work they can be proud of.

- **Share information.** Let them know some of the strategic goals, marketplace issues, difficult challenges, and other "big picture" forces that are the larger context of the project. Let them know that their limited contributions are tied to a higher purpose.

- **Do not micromanage their work.** Micromanaging sends this message: "I don't trust you to do this without my looking over your shoulder." Micromanaging is the opposite of respect.

- **Honor their family and community obligations.** Take the time to find out how the project will conflict with these important obligations and then do your best to help volunteers rearrange their project work and schedule as needed.

2. Protect them from administrivia and arbitrary rules.

Specifically you can:

- **Protect them from having to complete reports, attend meetings or participate in senior management "dog and pony shows"** that do not directly contribute to the quality of their work. Instead you, as project manager, can submit the report, attend the meeting, etc. on behalf of the volunteer. A quick, informal conversation with the volunteer may be all that's needed to prep you for "standing in" for them to complete these chores.

- **Let them choose their own work hours and work days.**

- **Let them to choose their own workplace.** Specifically, if they want to work off site and there is no compelling reason to be in the office or at the job site, encourage them to work wherever they choose.

- **Encourage them to let you know when anyone in your organization asks them to do something that does not directly contribute to the quality of their assigned project work.** Then take the necessary action to eliminate or otherwise protect them from this request.

3. Provide detailed, widely-circulated, career-enhancing feedback on their performance.

Specifically you can:

- **Tell them explicitly when they are doing a great job.** Let them know exactly what they did, in detail, that you appreciate.

- **Document, in writing, their specific contributions.** Then make sure this documentation is shared with 1) your senior management, 2) their senior management, 3) their personnel file, performance reviewers, etc.

- **Invite them to any celebrations, parties, lunches, retreats and any other** social or semi-social events that honor the contributions of the project team. (But make sure these are optional. They should be able to opt out of these gatherings if they choose to do so!)

- **Point the spotlight at volunteers and make sure they they are recognized and applauded for their work.** When the time comes to formally roll out the project results, make sure volunteers share the stage with you. Better yet, get out of the spotlight and let it shine on the volunteers who gave their time and energy to help the project succeed.

In introducing his book, *Drive: The Surprising Truth About What Motivates Us*, bestselling author Daniel Pink says "The secret to high performance and satisfaction—at work, at school, and at home—is the deeply human need to direct our own lives, to learn and create new things, and to do better by ourselves and our world."

Whether paid staff or unpaid volunteers, the people we want to have on our project teams — the creative, high-performing professionals who will help us create great results — aren't motivated so much by money as they are by what Pink refers to as "autonomy, mastery, and purpose." The strategies outlined above will help your project team members achieve all of these.

ONE SIMPLE THING TO IMPROVE PROJECTS OR PM (AN ANTHOLOGY)

In November of 2011 **I invited visitors to my main PM web site and other PM discussion sites to share "one simple thing..." that could improve projects and/or project management (PM).** Many smart people with lots of different PM experiences took the time to think about, then respond to, this invitation.

This free e-book anthology is a collection of their responses. It includes:

- Full-blown articles by guest bloggers published on my website

- Comments by my website's visitors

- Comments posted on LinkedIn's "PMChat" group

- Comments posted on this discussion on Focus (Focus.com).

My heartfelt "Thanks!" to all of those who were kind enough to create and share their thoughtful responses to this challenge! In fact, their compiled wisdom proved of such great value that this little e-book is now required reading in my online PM class for Franklin University!

I hope you find this anthology to be a thought-provoking and valuable resource. *Enjoy!*

- Download the *free mobi* file, One Simple Thing... for your **Kindle** (http://michaelgreer.biz/one-simple-thing/One-Simple-Thing-to-Improve-Projects-or-PM.mobi)

- Download the *free epub* file, One Simple Thing... for your **Nook, iPad, or other epub reader** (http://michaelgreer.biz/one-simple-thing/One-Simple-Thing-to-Improve-Projects-or-PM.epubhttp:/michaelgreer.biz/one-simple-thing/One-Simple-Thing-to-Improve-Projects-or-PM.epub)

- Download the *free PDF* file, One Simple Thing... (http://michaelgreer.biz/one-simple-thing/One-Simple-Thing-to-Improve-Projects-or-PM.pdf)

HOW TO SURVIVE FAMILY PROJECTS: 5 PM BEST PRACTICES

If you're reading this book, you're probably aware of the power of project management (PM) to bring order to potentially chaotic human endeavors. Organizations everywhere apply tried-and-true PM practices to get higher quality finished products, more quickly, and with less pain and frustration than if no PM were applied. In short, PM works almost anywhere where there are formal relationships among team members: businesses, governments, not-for-profits, etc.

Still, **there's one organization in which we spend much of our time**

that is not generally regarded as a candidate for PM techniques: the family. Seen through the lens of PM, a family can appear to be a random collection of informal, emotionally-charged relationships whose team members struggle mightily for control, power, recognition, autonomy, or simply to avoid work and avoid spending money. It is within this context that family reunions, weddings, home repair & improvement, landscaping, graduation parties and countless other domestic projects are undertaken by families. Some families are more successful than others in emerging from these efforts with their affections intact. Many complete such projects with permanent scars to relationships that must still, somehow, last a lifetime.

So how might your family avoid such self-inflicted wounds? **Below are 5 PM "best practices" that could help your family handle its next project more effectively.** (Note: You might also apply these to other unofficial project teams made up of close friends, volunteers, or anyone with whom you'd like to maintain a healthy personal relationship after the project is completed.)

Five PM Best Practices for Family Projects

1. Be clear about your priorities & how this project aligns with them.

Ask: Considering all the projects we need to complete, is this the right time to work on this?... to spend money this way?... to expend the effort? ... to take the time?

Consider this family project scenario:

Family Members: The family consists of two parents and three children. Both parents are working professionals who make a good income but are often busy with their careers. The eldest son is grown, newly married and generally helpful and supportive of his parents and their goals, though he sometimes spends extended hours at work building his new career.

Their daughter is currently living at home, but has recently finished college and is soon to be married. A wedding date has been set and the father of the bride has declared he wants to give her a beautiful, memorable wedding. Their youngest son is in 7th grade, a good athlete who enjoys participating in sports and other extracurricular activities.

Competing Projects:

- A complete kitchen remodel — Both parents enjoy cooking and share meal-preparation responsibilities. As a result, both are eager to remodel their ancient kitchen, which suffers from worsening plumbing problems.

- The daughter's wedding — This will be a major family event that is "… beautiful, memorable…"

- A new car for Mom — Mom's car is aging, sometimes failing, and generally racking up bills. Fortunately, when the car is unusable Mom has been taking the local bus to and from her office downtown. This adds time to her commute, but is tolerable. The couple wants to investigate electric or hybrid alternatives, so some research must precede the new car purchase.

Applying the Questions:

After a long discussion, Mom & Dad decide to endure their aging kitchen and Mom's aging car for a while longer in order to give their daughter the wedding of her dreams. They've resolved to devote lots of time, energy and money to making it a success.

The PM Lesson that Applies:

There's no point in trying to work together on a project unless all the players agree that 1) it's truly important and 2) it's the best possible use of money and time at this moment. Here's why: To complete a project, a family typically draws upon shared, and limited, resources (money, work space, equipment, tools, etc.). In addition, each family member will be spending time that he or she could choose to spend elsewhere. Because they are essentially volunteers and not employees, family members must decide willingly whether to contribute their time and their portion of any shared resources. In short, **they are free to choose among lots of options, so "they gotta wanna do it!" Unless they agree that the project is a top priority, they probably won't contribute their best.** Or worse, they could grouchily sabotage the project or simply walk away completely.

2. Have a clear project charter that is supported by everyone who matters.

Ask: Have we specified exactly what the outcome (finished product) should be?... should do?

Ask: What are our limits (boundaries) re: money?... time?... effort/days or hours?

Applying the Questions to the Scenario:

Before they speak to their daughter, Mom and Dad sit down and decide what the "upper limits" of their funding can be for the wedding. And they also discuss, in fairly detailed terms, how much effort and time they expect to spend themselves, individually, given the demands of their careers and support required for their younger son's school activities. After they are clear about their own definitions of the wedding boundaries and their respective roles, they sit down with their daughter and begin to sketch out her vision for the wedding. They ask her to imagine the entire event in vivid detail and then they help her identify some options for those things that might cost more money or take much more time than is available. Finally, Mom craftily decides — "just to help me remember everything" — that she will create a list of these options, limitations and agreements and then share copies of her list with her husband and daughter so their joint decisions are gently, but firmly, documented.

The PM Lesson that Applies:

When the "project" of this wedding planning is finally up and running, other members of the wedding party, as well as outside vendors (like photographer, caterer, musicians, etc.), will be joining the "project team." **Each new person who joins will bring a new bundle of creative ideas.** And each new idea, while it may thrill the bride if implemented, has the potential to impact the time, effort, and money required, as well as the quality of the overall finished product (the wedding itself). **Without clear boundaries** as captured in Mom's "help me remember" list (This is essentially the team's informal project charter.), **there would be no way to distinguish ideas that are "outside the scope" versus those that are welcome** enhancements that fit within the project boundaries.

3. Identify all the stakeholders and involve them in making project plans & defining outcomes.

Ask: Have we named everyone who can specify the work to be done and then actually do the work (or hire it done)?

Ask: Have we involved everyone who has the power to reject our results, complain about our results, or cause us to redo all or part of our work?

Ask: Have we made project plans that include 1) clearly defined results, 2) a list of tasks (chores to be performed) and 3) deadlines for completing tasks/chores?

Applying the Questions to the Scenario:

As they begin thinking about the chores to be done, Mom, Dad and our bride start to consider which family members might be able or willing to do certain chores. In her professional role, Mom has sometimes had to work with local venues (country club, hotel ballrooms, etc.) and vendors to organize public events. The elder son has organized several successful media promotions on behalf of his company, so he knows photographers and video people who might capture the wedding for posterity. One of the bride's friends has a sister who is a caterer and also has connections among local musicians who might provide entertainment.

And then there's Grandma: Our bride is her favorite granddaughter, so Grandma is fairly bursting with energy (and ideas) about this wedding and she is determined to get involved in "a big way." Finally, our bride has distinct and passionate ideas about the wedding theme, colors, and other matters of style. In contrast, Dad seems a bit overwhelmed by the rapidly emerging list of chores and details regarding the design and social dimensions. So he has decided to simply step back, do what he's assigned and "write 'reasonable' checks as needed." In sum, the family appears to have identified specific people who will be able to "own" most of the important parts of the project.

All these people, with their varying interests, experiences, hopes, and dreams must now sit down together and come up with a project plan that includes 1) a fairly detailed description of the wedding, 2) a list of chores to be done and 3) deadlines (dates) for completing these chores.

The PM Lesson that Applies:

Instead of simply jumping in and starting to work, it's best to step back and think about the talent, experience, preferences, and overall ability of potential team members to complete the project. At the same time, it's important, early on, to involve people that will have strong feelings about the results (e.g., our bride & Grandma) regardless of their abilities, because they could potentially reject, rethink, and otherwise derail the project. **By getting all these people around the same table,** we can create a plan that is a reflection of their abilities, interests, hopes, and biases. In short, a shared "high resolution" vision (well thought-out & argued-through) is more likely to be successfully (and peacefully!) executed.

4. Openly declare project roles & responsibilities, then make sure all agree.

Ask: Exactly who will perform each of the chores required to complete the project? Does each responsible person agree? Better yet, did each responsible person help define her own work process and agree that she could handle this assignment?

Applying the Questions to the Scenario:

Based on the skills and interests of our family team, we've divided up the chores as follows:

- Mom will identify one or two potential venues that fit the budget and then sign a contract with the final choice.

- The bride will identify & finalize who will make up the wedding party, invitation list, etc.

- The bride will finalize dresses, color schemes for the venue, etc.

- Elder son will identify and interview potential photographers and videographers, then contract with whomever is chosen.

- Dad will be available for miscellaneous assignments, "go for" chores and writing checks.

- Bride's friend will work with her sister to come up with a menu for the wedding and some choices for the entertainment.

- Grandma will support the bride, Dad and Mom as needed in miscellaneous chores.

The PM Lesson that Applies:

Project chores should be assigned based on interests, willingness, abilities, and project need. The list of assignments above is based on 1) declared interests of volunteers, 2) skills and experience and 3) what needs to be done to complete the project. Given that this is a family project, it would be difficult to go much deeper into creating a detailed task list without offending the volunteers and making them feel micromanaged. (However, going to such detail could make sense in a more formal or complex family project.)

5. Align team members' authority (power to act, make decisions, spend money) with their particular responsibilities.

Ask: Does each person to whom a chore is assigned have the authority to take independent action to complete the chore, make decisions related to quality or work process, spend money, and inspect or reject the inputs of helpers or suppliers? If not, who does have the necessary authority and how will this be used?

Applying the Questions to the Scenario:

Below is our list of authority/responsibilities as negotiated, right up front, with everyone on the wedding team.

- Wedding venue: Mom recommends, bride approves overall choice, Dad approves cost.

- Wedding party, invitation list, color schemes, dresses, etc.: Everyone recommends, bride approves aesthetics, Dad approves costs.

- Photographer/videographer: Elder son recommends, bride approves choice, Dad approves cost.

- Menu/food: Bride & bride's friend recommend, bride approves choice, Dad approves cost.

- Entertainment: Bride & bride's friend recommend, bride approves choice, Dad approves cost.

- Miscellaneous matters of aesthetics, style, tradition, etc.: Grandma, Mom, & anyone else recommends to bride. Bride approves.

Note that this list clearly distinguishes recommenders from approvers. This is important because as people become more involved in their roles it's easy to become swept away with enthusiasm for "my recommended approach" and become heavily invested in seeing it implemented. But as the list above makes clear, input is welcome, but our bride and Dad have final approval.

The PM Lesson that Applies:

Decisions, decisions, decisions! This wedding, like so many family projects, will be made up of lots of little decisions that may seem trivial individually, but when taken together can have a huge impact on the success of the project. More importantly, **how all these "little" decisions are made can either strengthen or permanently damage family relationships when the project is finally over.** For example, if our bride feels she was bullied into a decision, by-passed, or ignored, she's not likely to forget it soon. Alternately, if the bride over-rules a decision or vetoes someone's work capriciously, after they've worked hard to make what they believed was an important contribution, they can be hurt and remain so for years to come.

So it's important to define clearly, right up front, who is 1) responsible for doing the various chores [see list in #4, above], 2) who can make recommendations (i.e., have their opinions heard) and 3) who will make the final "go, no go" decision (i.e., who will approve). In this way, it will be less likely that someone "takes over" a chore or imposes a decision through sheer force of personality.

Conclusion

While there are lots more formal PM best practices that could be stretched to fit family projects, the five above are likely to have the greatest positive impact. Indeed, simply putting these five to work may challenge the diplomacy of any family project leader. If you do decide to try these on your next family project, by all means do so gently and with a sense of humor. What's more, you might want to admit to everyone on your "team" that you're only suggesting these tried-and-true PM formalities in order to make sure you all remain on speaking terms when the project is finally completed.

Good luck! And remember to **share plenty of hugs** along the way!

10 PODCASTS TO INSPIRE YOUR FAMILY "TEAM"

Here is a list of 10 free podcasts from the Inspired Project Teams archives that you can use to help inspire your family project team. As you listen to each (or read the blog post) simply substitute the word "family" for "team," and think about how you could apply the insights to your next big family project.

1. Shift from Drama to Empowerment

In his book *The Power of TED*, David Emerald compares two very different ways of being: The Dreaded Drama Triangle (or DDT) versus The Empowerment Dynamic (or TED). We apply these to project teams. *(URL: http://www.inspiredprojectteams.com/?p=580)*

2. Let Go of Perfectionism

Are you driven to perfection? ... or simply driven crazy? This post/podcast provides suggestions for project managers and team leaders about how they can let go of perfectionism and improve their results. *(URL: http://www.inspiredprojectteams.com/?p=276)*

3. Consciously Choose Your Attitude

A project team's attitude can make or break the project. In this post you learn how you can consciously choose your attitude instead of simply allowing it to overtake you as a collection of random feelings. *(URL: http://www.inspiredprojectteams.com/?p=1026)*

4. Accept What Is

You must first accept a difficult situation for what it is before you can handle it effectively. Accept it, see it clearly without denial and hand-wringing, and then you can take appropriate action. *(URL: http://www.inspiredprojectteams.com/?p=752)*

5. Learn to Be Optimistic... Learn to Succeed

"Cognitive therapy works [by changing] explanatory style from pessimistic to optimistic [providing]... skills for talking to yourself when you fail." – M. Seligman – This post/podcast applies this to project teams. *(URL: http://www.inspiredprojectteams.com/?p=507)*

6. Take Charge... Stop Playing the Victim

You create your own experience...[&] you cannot change what you do not acknowledge." – Dr. Phil McGraw – Post/podcast focuses on how project teams can accept responsibility for bad results & take charge. *(URL: http://www.inspiredprojectteams.com/?p=176)*

7. Get High on Kindness

"Kindness extended, received, or observed beneficially impacts the physical health and feelings of everyone involved!" — Wayne Dyer *(URL: http://www.inspiredprojectteams.com/?p=97)*

8. Listen, Understand, Collaborate

"Habit 5: Seek First to Understand, Then to be Understood." – Stephen Covey's Seven Habits of Highly Effective People – Audio examines why & how project teams should listen, understand, & collaborate. *(URL: http://www.inspiredprojectteams.com/?p=191)*

9. Get Excited... and Let It Show!

"Nothing great was ever achieved without enthusiasm." — Ralph Waldo Emerson *(URL: http://www.inspiredprojectteams.com/?p=193)*

10. Just Say No

While it might make sense for individuals to say "yes" to life as often as they can, there are critical moments when project teams have just gotta say "no!" Here's why & how... *(URL: http://www.inspiredprojectteams.com/?p=944)*

Conclusion

I've tried to use many of the ideas contained in these podcasts with my own family projects, with varying degrees of success. All-in-all, however, I know there's much of value here that can help you inspire your family teams to complete their projects more effectively and.... (dare I say it?) more lovingly! So give these a try!

PEACE OF MIND

If you're all crazy and agitated, you'll likely transmit this insanity to the rest of your project team. And worse, your work-related agitation is likely to follow you home, generally screwing up your personal life.

On the other hand, if you can acquire a centered, peaceful state of mind, there's a good chance you can help to calm things down on your project when things start to get tense.

This Part examines some of my favorite perspectives and specific techniques that can lead you to a more peaceful state of mind.

WHY YOU SHOULD TRUST YOUR JUDGMENT (YOUR "INNER WISDOM FILTER")

*(This book excerpt is from "The People Stuff: 10 Sets of Challenges to Inspire Teams" in **The Project Management Minimalist: Just Enough PM to Rock Your Projects!**)*

"A man should learn to detect and watch that gleam of light which flashes across his mind from within, more than the luster of the firmament of bards and sages... Trust thyself: every heart vibrates to that iron string."
— Ralph Waldo Emerson in **Self-Reliance**

"... the best in every business do what they have learned to do without questioning their abilities — they flat out trust their skills, which is why we call this high-performance state of mind the 'Trusting Mindset.' Routine access to the Trusting Mindset is what separates great performers from the rest of the pack."
— John Eliot in **Overachievement**

"Skill in any performance, whether it be in sports, in playing the piano, in conversation, or in selling merchandise, consists not in painfully and consciously thinking out each action as it is performed, but in relaxing, and letting the job do itself through you. Creative performance is spontaneous and 'natural' as opposed to self-conscious and studied."
— Maxwell Maltz in **Psycho-Cybernetics**

"By banishing doubt and trusting your intuitive feelings, you clear a space

for the power of intention to flow through."
— Wayne Dyer in ***The Power of Intention***

So, do you trust yourself — really trust yourself — to come up with that creative leap, that exactly appropriate solution, that powerful insight that maybe no one else can generate?

The message shared by all these great teachers... indeed, by many other great philosophers... is that **to achieve anything great you must trust that voice which lies deep within you and is trying to be heard.**

1. If I could see you right now, I'm guessing some of you who are reading this are rolling your eyes and judging this all as a bit fluffy, cosmic, new agey, or "woo woo!" Still, I'm willing to bet that you (or some people you respect) have used one of these expressions:

- "I just had a hunch that..."
- "I had this strong intuition about..."
- "I had to go with my gut... I just did what seemed right."
- "I had a strong feeling about this and I just decided to follow my heart."

Whether you call it a "hunch," an "intuition," a "gut feeling" or simply the unspoken nudging of your heart, you're talking about pretty much the same thing: that inner voice of wisdom that we all possess, but we all too often stifle. Sure, this inner voice we're talking about can be intangible and elusive. But I bet that if you had to do so, you could logically trace the origins of its judgments and choices. And this logical audit trail would prove to you that this inner voice is really quite worthy of your trust and respect.

Here's the deal: **Your intuitions, "gut feelings," and hunches are derived from and ultimately grounded in your unique life experiences, both good and bad. And because of this, they have behind them the solid proof of your reality.** To illustrate how all these experiences come together to generate solid, trustworthy judgments, I present to you the analogy of the common kitchen strainer. (Now stick with me, here... this is actually a pretty cool analogy!)

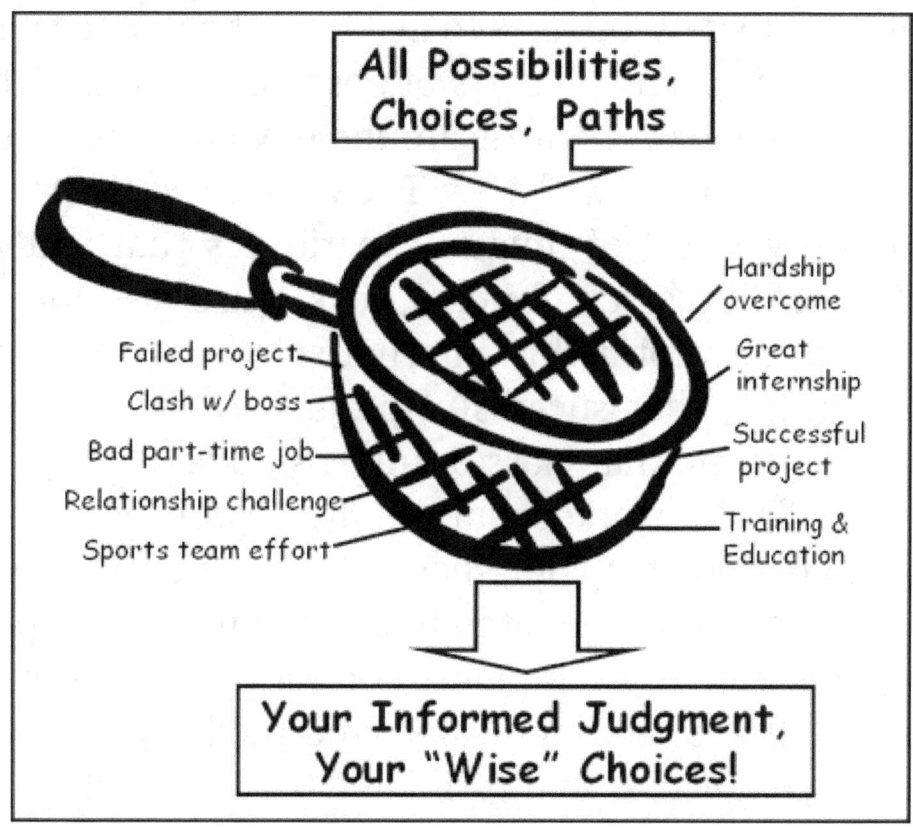

Your hard-earned Wisdom Filter

A kitchen strainer is made up of a whole bunch of strands of wire, criss-crossed to form a grid or a screen. Now let's say you don't have one of those fancy juice machines, but you want to mash up a bunch of fruit and extract the juice. You begin by cutting the fruit into pieces, then dump these pieces into the strainer. You then place the strainer over a bowl and push down on the fruit and mash it up until the juice runs into the bowl. The wire grid or screen of the strainer prevents all the seeds, stems, strands of bitter fibers, and fruit skins from coming through. The only thing you get in your bowl is the juice essence that you wanted. All that other stuff can be thrown out (or added to you favorite fiber-dense muffin dough!).

Your Inner Wisdom Filter

Your inner voice (i.e., your judgment) operates pretty much like that kitchen strainer! Let's say you have to make a difficult decision and don't have time to think about it. All sorts of possibilities and pertinent facts and constraints and outcomes rattle around in your brain. Your "internal strainer" is activated to deal with this. The wires in your internal strainer are made up of a vast set of unique experiences that you've acquired over your lifetime. Successes, failures, joys, miseries, and all sorts of life events combine to form this internal screening mechanism. That horrible job you had, that successful project, that challenge on your high school sports team, that class or internship you took, that difficult relationship you finally worked out — all these events comprise the unique strainer that creates your special judgments. And when all the possible solutions and issues related to a problem are dumped into that strainer, the good stuff — a unique and powerful judgment — emerges. It's a judgment that's automatically informed by all of your life experiences. And, as such, it's powerful and trustworthy!

Still skeptical? Consider some real-life examples:

- A badly battered and bleeding patient is wheeled into **the emergency room at a hospital.** The on-call physician takes charge and begins diagnosing and treating the patient at a whirlwind pace. A life is at stake… there's no time to stop and think. Instead, the filter of the doctor's unique experiences (med school classes, internships, time served in the military, previous years working in an ER) — this filter kicks in to quickly sort and choose among possible treatment strategies. Appropriate action is taken and a life is saved.

- **A wise tribal elder** is called on to mediate a dispute between neighbors. She doesn't need to consult legal texts or put the matter to a vote. She simply considers the situation in light of her years and years of life experiences and knowledge of the tribe, then makes her recommendation. The unique situation and options are filtered through her experiences and a trustworthy recommendation emerges.

- Your grandpa has been making his **prize winning chili** for many years. Somewhere back in his dim past, he used a recipe. But over time he's learned from making bad batches and good batches that a little more of this vegetable and a little of that spice added at just the right time in the cooking process results in chili that gets rave reviews. He'd be hard pressed to tell you exactly how he does it. The grid of his internal experiences simply produces high quality judgments automatically throughout the cooking process, while he's busy cutting up vegetables and stirring.

- Then there's **those fine artists we all admire.** They've been highly trained in brush selection and handling, paint mixing, composition, and so on. But when they start painting, they simply flow into the work. They allow the subject that inspires them to be strained through the grid of their training and unique sensibilities to create something that is beautiful and new. They trust their judgment.

- And finally, consider **the simple act of parallel parking your car.** As you align your tires to the curb and ease into the parking space, a thousand automatic muscle memories are activated to press the accelerator and the brake pedals at just the right times, turn the steering wheel just so, and scan your mirrors to get feedback on how you are doing. You don't tell your brain how to integrate all this hand-eye movement. Your internal filter simply takes in all the possibilities, sorts through them to figure out what really matters, and provides you with the judgment to park quickly and allow the other cars who are waiting for you to finish parking to be on their way.

The bottom line: You already HAVE trustworthy judgment! It's impossible to live your life without activating — and trusting — this judgment a thousand times a day! So why not really embrace it? Why not learn to trust your judgment whole-heartedly when you're making all those difficult professional decisions? Remember, deep down, you already know what you need to know!

Now let's apply all this to project management.

Reflections

Reflect on these questions:

- What are some of the complex things you do without thinking? (Consider sports, brain games, coaching, sifting & sorting through things, inspecting, quality assurance?)

- If you had to do so, would you be able to dissect one of these complex abilities and show each skill and bit of knowledge and experience which makes you able to do this thing so well?

- When have you been under pressure to produce a fast decision on a complex issue? How did you fare? Was it a good decision? If you had to, could you defend it based on your experiences, skills, and training?

- What are some areas of your job or career where you might be overthinking things? Could you begin to relax and trust your judgment in these areas?

Team Challenges

Ask your team:

- Think about the projects you have worked on. When was the last time you had a really powerful experience of "I told you so!"

- Could this "I told you so..." event have been avoided if you had "spoken up," honoring that inner voice that knew better?

- Look back on your accumulated experiences and expertise. These are the sources of your judgment. How might we, as a project team, better leverage your judgment on our projects?

- What do you need from senior managers or project managers that would enable you to more confidently "trust yourself?"

Project Manager Challenges

- Take a few minutes to review each of your team members' resumes, job histories, and project track records. Look for signs of untapped wisdom.

- What parts of our projects are in need of some of the wisdom and judgment that our people may already have, but aren't using?

- Thinking about each team member and his or her experiences and expertise, ask yourself these questions:

  ◦ Are we really using this person's judgment to the fullest extent?

  ◦ Do we create a safe environment in which this person can apply their judgment?

  ◦ Do I need to try to prove to this person that they can trust their judgment by pointing out their long history of successes and good decisions?

  ◦ What can I do to help this person develop the confidence to more fully trust his or her judgment?

  ◦ What obstacles can I remove that are impeding them from exercising their judgment or are making them overly cautious?

10 SPECIFIC ACTIONS THAT CAN HELP YOU BECOME HAPPIER

In this article (also available as a free audio podcast — http://www.inspiredprojectteams.com/?p=1122), I share 10 specific actions that I've taken to create more happiness in my life. Am I always true to these practices? No, unfortunately. But the more often I am able to follow them, the happier I seem to be. You might want to try some of these yourself

1. Turn off the local news; it's not real.

Think about it. News production is a business. News producers must create powerful headlines that generate a sense of urgency on the part of viewers or listeners. They want big, bold, sensational announcements that scream nervously about fires, murders, local indiscretions by public figures... all to attract a large audience. If it's nasty and ugly and sensational, we're going to hear about it. To make matters worse, these kinds of stories are comparatively easy to get. Journalists can simply listen in on the local police scanners, follow the police or fire department to the scene of the latest crime or accident, and pick up that sensational story. So it's easy for broadcasters to bury us in this drek! Yet, at the same time, there are countless little acts of kindness in neighborhoods everywhere that go unreported. What's more, there are employees who labor quietly to create a great new product, or go that extra mile to serve their customers, or otherwise make their anonymous positive contributions to make the world a better place. But most of this positive energy goes unnoticed by local news producers.

The result: You come home from a long, hard day at work, turn on local news, and a glut of negative energy pours over you. You wallow in bad events that simply aren't real for you, your family, or the people in your neighborhood! Ultimately you begin to feel a little uneasy, sad or angry. If you aren't careful, this stuff begins to cast a dark shadow over your whole life. But you don't have to let this happen! You can do what I do: I turn off my local news and go out and enjoy a walk in my neighborhood or call a friend or relative and say Hi or whatever! I do anything other than sit through all that bad news. (What about the local weather, you ask? No worries. I get my local weather, updated every few minutes, from the internet!)

2. Turn off the national & world news; it's not real either.

The same business dynamics related to local news apply to the national and world news. And worse yet, with national and world journalism, the scale of the bad news is typically much grander. The bad behaviors of public figures are said to have world-wide implications. The wars (there are always wars, right?) and acts of inhumanity are captured in gory detail. And it is implied that the local disaster on the other side of the world could soon apply to you, in your neighborhood. Meanwhile, in nations all over the world, public officials, citizens, and workers labor quietly to do their jobs as best they can and generate countless acts of kindness that go uncelebrated. So again, I suggest this: Turn off the national and world news, go outside and look around. There's a good chance that all that bad news that was so compelling as it poured into your home is simply not a reality in your back yard, in your neighborhood, in you family, or among your friends. And if it's not in these places, then it's not real to you. So why let it shape your thoughts and your mood?

Here's a challenge: Stop watching local, national, and world news for one solid week. At the end of the week, tune in to a news broadcasts and see how you feel. If you're like me, you'll be shocked at the amount of negative energy these things spew at you. And you'll probably quickly turn them off again!

Remember these words from Marcus Aurelius: "Such as are your habitual thoughts, such also will be the character of your mind, for the soul is dyed by the thoughts." So the question is: Do you want your soul to be dyed the color of bad news or the color of the countless good deeds that are happening all around you?

3. Turn off political talk shows; they simply pick at wounds.

Are you a fan of Rachel Maddow or Rush Limbaugh? Of Glenn Beck or Keith Olberman? Whatever your political orientation, the shows hosted by these people (and many others like them) typically have the same effect on you as a viewer or a listener: They cause you to feel angry, excited, sad, cynical, self-righteous, or some other extreme (and usually not pleasant) emotion. Like the news producers discussed earlier, they are in the business of getting people to attend to their broadcasts — of getting people to react and talk about them and bring their friends and relatives to the next broadcast. And to do so, they push your buttons, stir up your prejudices, link together truths and half-truths with strong opinions and commentary, and generally raise your blood pressure.

I used to tell myself that time spent with such shows was time spent "informing" myself of key issues. But after a while, I started to realize that I wasn't simply being informed; I was being needlessly agitated. I was developing a gloomy consciousness that the people in charge of all the institutions of our country, especially its political leaders and elected officials, were either corrupt or bumbling... and certainly not worthy of my trust. I suddenly realized that these shows actually left me less meaningfully informed, often confused, and almost always more anxious about the world around me.

So these days, I inform myself about the key issues of the day by looking for information on my own terms. Give me the web and a browser and I create my own body of facts on issues by examining such truly balanced websites as ProCon.org or Project Vote Smart or FactCheck.org. While these aren't as entertaining as the political talk shows, they provide solid information that I acquire and digest for myself!

So, if you're a fan of those ranting... er, talking... heads on radio or TV, try this simple experiment. The next time you finish one of their programs, find a quiet place to sit for a few minutes and pay close attention to your feelings or the energy field you are experiencing. Are you happier? ... more peaceful? ... more hopeful? If you're like me, you'll soon realize that spending time with these shows can be toxic to your happiness. So turn them off.

(*An aside:* A basic principle of good management is that a manager's authority should equal her responsibility. Every time I hear one of these talking heads ranting about what one of our leaders should be doing, I see that they are using their authority to broadcast their opinions to all of us, while they have absolutely no responsibility for bringing about the changes they are calling for. I can't help wondering what their grand pronouncements would sound like if these people actually had to do the hard, and often thankless, work of governing, building consensus, and simply trying to get things done.)

4. Connect with positive media that enlighten & challenge you.

So, given that so many news and talk shows generate so much unhappiness, where can you turn to find media that enlightens, challenges, and contributes to your happiness? Good news! The web is full of such media, much of it entirely free. If you were to look through my MP3 player right now, you'd find many programs from the sources listed below. I listen to these while exercising, standing in line shopping, or whenever I need a little inspiration.

- Brian Johnson's PhilosophersNotes — "The Biggest Ideas from 100 of The Most Influential Books On Personal Growth In 20 Minutes Or Less" (See my testimonial video about these on YouTube.)

- Oprah's Soul Series Webcasts — "Each week Oprah or guest hosts... sits down with leading spiritual thinkers, teachers and authors to talk about matters of the soul."

- LearnOutLoud.com — Thousands and thousands of audios and videos and podcasts. Classical books, contemporary great thinkers & self-improvement. Much of it is entirely free!

- TED Talks — "Riveting talks by remarkable people, free to the world."

- LibriVox — "Acoustical liberation of books in the public domain."

- The Best Free Training — This website & blog can help you find great free online or downloadable courses that will challenge and stretch you! *(Disclosure: I research & post all the items listed at this website. - MG)*

The list of sources above only begins to scratch the surface of the vast collections of positive, uplifting media that are available to you — mostly for free — on the 'net. So turn off your TV or radio and connect with something positive!

5. Create something, grow something, nurture someone, and use your signature strengths.

As I've said elsewhere, the following two quotes are powerful influences on my day-to-day life:

- "If you bring forth what is inside you, what you bring forth will save you. If you don't bring forth what is inside you, what you don't bring forth will destroy you." – *Jesus*

- "Your purpose is to act on the resources God gives you. If God gives you a bucket of fish, you have to distribute those fish. If you don't, they're going to rot, attract a bunch of flies, and start stinking up your soul." – *Russell Simmons*

So here's the deal: Whether you happen to feel it right now or not, you should know that God (or Source energy or your Muse or whatever) is in every one of us generating a powerful need to "bring forth" our talents and experiences in a unique way to create something, grow something, nurture something, and use what Dr. Martin Seligman calls our "signature strengths." Seligman says (and his years of clinical research prove) that using these strengths is the key to happiness. According to Seligman: "I do not believe that you should devote overly much effort to correcting your weaknesses. Rather, I believe that the highest success in living and the deepest emotional satisfaction comes from building and using your signature strengths." (This is from Seligman's Authentic Happiness — To learn more about your unique signature strengths, go to http://www.authentichappiness.org, sign up for your free membership, and work through the VIA Signature Strengths Questionnaire.)

So if you are feeling less than happy... even anxious... you need to ask yourself: "What can I create, what can I help grow or develop, who might I nurture to make the world a better place? And how can I share my signature strengths?" Answer these questions, take action based on your answers, and become happier.

6. Exercise. Move.

This is a truly simple cure for unhappiness that I discovered many years ago: To change what you are thinking (i.e., unhappy, restless, anxious thoughts), change what you are doing. There is something about getting out of the office, away from the desk, off the couch and stepping outside that immediately starts working on your mood. Your entire body becomes engaged in movement, you see new sites, smell new smells, feel the wind in your face, and forget your troubles. When you exercise or move you automatically shift your mental perspective and start concentrating on the movement itself, whether it's walking, running, dancing, lifting weights, operating your bike — whatever. Fresh air moves into your lungs, stale air is exhaled. Blood circulates and floods your brain cells with fresh oxygen and nutrients. Your natural happiness chemical, serotonin, is released. Maybe even a little adrenalin flows into your bloodstream as a natural pick-me-up. In short, a quick way to feel better is to get moving. A good way to keep feeling better over the long haul is to develop a regular habit of exercise. But you've heard all this before, right? So... what are you waiting for?

7. Perform a simple act of kindness.

This wonderful quote from Wayne Dyer says it all:

"The positive effect of kindness on the immune system and on the increased production of serotonin in the brain has been proven in research studies. Serotonin is a naturally occurring substance in the body that makes us feel more comfortable, peaceful, and even blissful. ... most anti-depressants... stimulate the production of serotonin chemically, helping to ease depression. Research has shown that a simple act of kindness directed toward another improves the functioning of the immune system and stimulates the production of serotonin in both the recipient of the kindness and the person extending the kindness. Even more amazing is that persons observing the act of kindness have similar beneficial results. Imagine this! Kindness extended, received, or observed beneficially impacts the physical health and feelings of everyone involved!" — Wayne Dyer in The Power of Intention

So look around. Who would benefit from a simple act of kindness? Perform that act and become happier!

8. Stop complaining.

We've all heard the recent findings about the amazing plasticity of the human brain. The good news is that it can rewire itself after being injured, stretch itself in new ways to meet new demands, and generally adapt to almost anything we ask it to adapt to. The bad news is that if you continually point your amazing plastic brain at a sad or miserable event in you life, you develop the ability to relive this event over and over again in your own version of "high definition!" Worse yet, telling your sad story over and over to your friends and families eventually gives it the strength of a personal myth or legend that defines you and how others see you. Not only do you relive the misery, but everyone else gets to share it with you again and again. The result: Instead of having a rotten thing happen to you once and then be over and done with, you become trapped in the rottenness by telling and retelling your story. And your plastic brain accommodates this self-destructive urge by allocating plenty of neurons and brain real estate to your epic suffering. Is this really what you want? To poison your consciousness repeatedly... to allow the event that offended or injured you to have everlasting life in your consciousness and the consciousness of those around you? I don't think so! So... stop complaining. Let it go, already! And get a little happier.

9. Express gratitude frequently.

I've often heard it said, quite wisely, that you cannot be angry or resentful while expressing gratitude. True feelings of gratitude simply displace these negative emotions. In fact, researchers studying happiness have found clinical evidence that cultivating gratitude contributes measurably to happiness. One specific practice identified by researchers is the "gratitude visit." In this practice, you have one week to write and then deliver a letter of gratitude in person to someone who had been especially kind to you but had never been properly thanked. Another specific practice is called "Three good things in life." In this practice, every night for one week you write down three things that went well each day and provide a causal explanation for each good thing (i.e., describe why it happened). Practicing both these exercises has been clinically shown to increase levels of happiness in those who practice them. Based on these findings and the work of Martin Seligman (author of Authentic Happiness), the practice of creating a Gratitude Journal is becoming a widely accepted method of increasing your overall happiness. So look for reasons to be grateful, look for opportunities to express this gratitude, and then do so frequently!

(For lots of details, references, etc., see my series on The Science of Happiness on my blog, The Best Free Training [http://www.bestfreetraining.net/?p=191]. Or check out my Inspired Project Teams posts/podcasts Train Yourself to be Happier [http://www.inspiredprojectteams.com/?p=230] and Learn to Be Optimistic... Learn to Succeed [http://www.inspiredprojectteams.com/?p=507].)

10. Practice mindfulness and mindful meditation.

By "mindfulness and mindful meditation" I mean the secular practice (not particularly religious or spiritual) of simply being in this moment. By learning to be more fully here and now you can shed the happiness-killing habits of ruminating over past troubles or fearing future problems. And the beauty of it is, everyone already knows how to find this present moment! It's right here, available for us all to experience. Whether you formally practice mindful meditation or not, you've no doubt already experienced some moments of being fully mindful such as these:

• Sitting in a garden watching a flower

- Admiring a sunset or a cloud formation

- Listening intently to a favorite piece of music

- Writing a poem or story

- Painting a picture

- Intensely running or biking or playing basketball

- Listening to the sounds of birds chattering or waves lapping the shoreline

- Simply staring into space and discovering a few minutes of tranquility in what seems like a timeless and formless place

If you've ever engaged in one of these practices, allowing thoughts of the past and future to disappear revealing a few minutes of pure "here and now," you've practiced mindfulness. And one of the most powerful ways of increasing your overall level of peace and happiness is to build on these moments of mindfulness — to extend them so they become a larger part of your life. I discussed all of this and the work of Jon Kabat-Zinn in helping millions cultivate mindfulness in an earlier blog post and podcast titled Practice Mindfulness (http://www.inspiredprojectteams.com/?p=766). In that post I shared my own experience with the practice of mindfulness through mindful meditation:

"Every morning I meditate for about 20 minutes before I start my day. After doing this for a couple of years, I have found two powerful benefits. First, I seem to have developed the ability to find this quiet mindful space and to call on it in the other parts of my life, when I'm not meditating. It's as though I always have a comfortable bench under a shade tree to which I can retreat for a few minutes when things are getting too frenzied out there on the sunny playing field of my life. Second, this mindfulness practice has lowered (yes, lowered) my tolerance to stress! I am no longer willing to put up with my mind spinning out of control dreading fictional futures or ranting about past horrors. When the noise starts, I can see it as it really is: just noise. And I witness it, and wait for it to pop like so many soap bubbles. I don't claim to be in perfect harmony, but all-in-all, my 20 minute daily mindfulness meditation practice is well worth the time spent!"

So how about it? Why not build on your already-present ability to "be here, be now" and start practicing mindful meditation for extended periods of time. It will help you become a more peaceful, satisfied, and happier person.

Footnote: The negative media discussed earlier (news and political talk shows) are powerful forces that work against your mindfulness and against your being in the present moment. They actually encourage you to spend time ruminating about past horrors and fearing future events. By turning these negative media off, and turning on the "here and now," you can truly increase your happiness.

Reflections

Reflect on these questions:

- Do you or your team members spend much time talking about bad news?

- What are some real, local good news events that have been happening in your community?

- What are some real, good news events in your team members' family lives?

- When people start talking about bad news, could you shift the discussion to the good community and family news?

- What are some positive media sources you engage frequently? Have you ever shared these with your team?

- Do you express gratitude frequently… especially so your team members can hear you?

- Do you and your project team members have opportunities to practice mindfulness and stay grounded in the present moment?

Team Challenges

Ask your team:

- Do we complain too much? (What do we get from this?)

- Do we spend time rehashing bad news or bad events? (What good news, personal or business, can we share?)

- To whom or about what might we express more gratitude?

- Do we have places in our work environment that we can go to practice a bit of meditation or get some energy-renewing exercise?

Project Manager Challenges

As project manager or team leader, you can set the tone for your team by becoming a role model who performs the specific actions that encourage happiness. For example, you can:

- Share how you are connecting with positive media that enlighten & challenge you.

- Share how you have discovered and are trying to use your signature strengths to create something, grow something, or nurture someone.

- Share ways you make time to exercise and move. (And you can help create time and places in the workplace to support exercise and movement.)

- Perform simple acts of kindness as often as you can.

- Express gratitude frequently.

- Practice mindfulness and being "here and now," by discouraging the rehashing of bad past events and discouraging the fearful thoughts of negative future possibilities. Instead, show how you keep focused on the present moment.

- Take a few minutes out of every work day to close your door or go to a quiet place and meditate.

You can also discourage the behaviors that work against happiness. Specifically, you can:

- Refuse to spend time talking about bad news and negative headlines.

- Refuse to spend time engaged in political debates and partisan rants.

- Stop complaining... and challenge your team members to turn every complaint into a recommendation for improvement of some sort.

MEDITATION FACT SHEET: SCIENTIFICALLY PROVEN BENEFITS AND A WHO'S WHO OF FAMOUS MEDITATORS

I'm calling this a "fact sheet" because instead of the usual paragraphs and paragraphs of prose, I'm providing a condensed summary of the following:

- **The Proven Benefits of Meditation** (scientifically studied & reported in respected journals)

- **A Who's Who of Meditators & Organizations** Who Encourage Meditation

To create this fact sheet, I've culled information from several bloggers, book authors, and websites. I've included links to all these so you can easily go to the original source for further details.

*[**NOTE:** In this fact sheet **I use the word "meditation" in its broadest sense to include any activity that helps you focus attention, step outside the stream of internal mental chatter and achieve what Dr. Herbert Benson refers to as "the relaxation response."** Examples of such activities include: repeating a mantra, mindfulness meditation, transcendental Meditation, Vipassana meditation, breath focus, Kripalu or Kundalini yoga, repetitive prayer, or even walking or jogging with a focus on regular footfalls.]*

The Proven Benefits of Meditation

According to an article at the Mayo Clinic website (http://www.mayoclinic.com/health/meditation/HQ01070), "meditation... results in enhanced physical and emotional well-being." This conservative website is careful to present its medical topics without a lot of hype. And its conclusions and recommendations are typically peer reviewed and use carefully chosen, scientifically-defensible descriptions. Regarding meditation, it states:

- "The emotional benefits of meditation include:
- Gaining a new perspective on stressful situations
- Building skills to manage your stress
- Increasing self-awareness
- Focusing on the present
- Reducing negative emotions

Meditation also might be useful if you have a medical condition, especially one that may be worsened by stress. ... some research suggests that meditation may help such conditions as:

- Allergies
- Anxiety disorders
- Asthma
- Binge eating
- Cancer
- Depression
- Fatigue

- Heart disease

- High blood pressure

- Sleep problems

- Substance abuse"

In his extensive article for io9, *The Science Behind Meditation and Why it Makes You Feel Better (http://io9.com/how-meditation-changes-your-brain-and-makes-you-feel-b-470030863)*, George Dvorsky reviews how meditation changes the brain and subsequently results in several health benefits. In addition, Dvorsky provides links to several scientific studies. Below are highlights from his article:

Changes to the Brain

- **"Higher levels of gyrification** — the "folding" of the cerebral cortex as a result of growth, which in turn may allow the brain to process information faster.

- **Larger hippocampal and frontal volumes of gray matter**, resulting in more positive emotions, the retention of emotional stability, and more mindful behavior (heightened focus

- **Diminished age-related effects** on gray matter and reduce cognitive decline

- **Decreased activity in default mode network activity and connectivity** — those undesirable brain functions responsible for lapses of attention and disorders such as anxiety, ADHD — and even the buildup of beta amyloid plaques in Alzheimer's disease.

- **Dramatic changes in electrical brain activity**, namely increased Theta and Alpha EEG activity, which is associated with wakeful and relaxed attention.

Health Benefits

- **An easier time sustaining voluntary attention**

- **Significant improvements in mindfulness and contemplative thoughts**, the alleviation of depressive symptoms, and boosts to working memory and sustained attention.

- **Significant reduction in stress** after just eight weeks of training

- **Increased levels of empathy**" [observed "live" during brain scans of meditators/non-meditators]

An article at Rodale.com, *6 Surprising Benefits of Meditation (http://www.rodale.com/health-benefits-meditation)*, lists **the following benefits of meditation** and provides many links to the scientific studies supporting them:

- "#1: Meditation can make you more productive.

- #2: It's good for surly teenagers.

- #3: Meditation helps you ditch the painkillers.

- #4: It'll keep you happy.

- #5: Meditate, combat hot flashes.

- #6: Your heart loves it when you meditate."

Finally, an article at the Medical News Today website titled *Yoga And Meditation Change Gene Response To Stress (http://www.medicalnewstoday.com/articles/113735.php)* reviews the recent work of Dr. Herbert Benson at his Benson-Henry Institute for Mind/Body Medicine. (Note: Dr. Benson wrote the landmark 1975 work, The Relaxation Response, which defined this response as the opposite of the "fight or flight" response.) The article presents this stunning finding:

"...mind body techniques like yoga and meditation that put the body in a state of deep rest known as the relaxation response, are capable of changing how genes behave in response to stress."

OK. One more time, because that's a very big deal!! The researchers found that yoga & meditation are

" … CAPABLE OF CHANGING HOW GENES BEHAVE IN RESPONSE TO STRESS…."

The article quotes Dr. Benson: "Now we've found how changing the activity of the mind can alter the way basic genetic instructions are implemented." And it quotes Dr. Towia Libermann, director of BIDMC Genomics Center and co-author of the study: **"This is the first comprehensive study of how the mind can affect gene expression, linking what has been looked on as a 'soft' science with the 'hard' science of genomics."**

A Who's Who of Meditators & Organizations Who Encourage Meditation

What follows is my "Who's Who" of meditators and organizations who practice, and encourage others to practice, meditation. My goal is to do **some significant name dropping** and show you that **many of the best, brightest, and most successful handle their stress with the help of meditation.** The list includes **everyone from rock stars to money market managers!** So you may be surprised at some of the names that appear here!

Online MBA News lists these 10 Big Companies That Promote Employee Meditation (http://www.onlinemba.com/blog/10-big-companies-that-promote-employee-meditation/)

- Apple

- Prentice Hall Publishing

- Google

- Nike

- AOL Time Warner

- McKinsey & Co.

- Yahoo

- Deutsche Bank

- Procter & Gamble

- HBO

The American Meditation Institute provides this long list of its corporate customers (http://www.americanmeditation.org/CorporateMeditation.aspx) at its website:

- "West Point Association of Graduates

- Berkshire Medical Center

- Albany Medical College, Family and Community Medicine Residency

- Albany Medical Center Bioethics Committee

- M.D. Anderson Cancer Center, Houston TX

- The Commonwealth Club of California

- Washington University Medical School, St. Louis MO

- Southern Illinois University at Edwardsville

- "The New York Times" Workshop: Yoga: The Power to Change Your Life" with Dean Ornish, M.D.

- University of Wisconsin School of Nursing, Madison WI

- University of Colorado Medical School Alternative Medicine Department

- College of St. Rose, Albany NY

- Hudson Valley Community College, North Greenbush NY

- Wesley Healthcare Center, Saratoga Springs NY

- The Cancer Center of Albany Med

- International Himalayan Yoga Teachers Association, Calgary, Canada

- New England Institute of Ayurvedic Medicine, Boston MA

- SUNY Empire State College, Saratoga Springs NY

- Rensselaer County ARC

- Baptist Retirement Center, Scotia NY

- Knolls Atomic Power Labs, Niskayuna and Ballston Spa NY"

In its article *Money Managers Find Benefits From Meditation (http://www.huffingtonpost.com/2013/04/17/money-managers-meditation-business-investment_n_3103986.html)*, Huffington Post names the following meditators:

- "**Ray Dalio**, founder of $130 billion hedge fund firm **Bridgewater Associates**

- **Bill Gross** of Pimco (**Bond king**)

- **Jason Voss**, 'a former money manager who now works for the **CFA Institute** and who has written a book about meditation and investment'"

The article concludes: "Meditation is likely to continue spreading among fund managers in the way it has in the rest of society: from hand to hand as something that people do and find helpful."

In *Sit. Breathe. Be a Better Leader (http://www.inc.com/articles/201110/ more-and-more-entrepreneurs-meditate-how-and-why-you-should- too.html)*, Inc.com identifies these entrepreneurial meditators and organizations:

"**Harley Murphy**, who heads the Ireland operations of BNY Mellon... Hip-hop mogul **Russell Simmons**... **Ray Dalio**, the 61-year-old founder of Bridgewater Associates, the world's biggest hedge fund.... **Bill Ford**'s a big advocate.... **Steve Jobs** was often associated with the practice. ... **Facebook, Ebay, and General Mills execs** are meditators. **Google** set up separate rooms so senior staff would be able to pursue it."

In *Bill Clinton Gets His Meditation On (http://www.mindbodygreen.com/ 0-5735/Bill-Clinton-Gets-His-Meditation-On.html)*, the MindBodyGreen website describes how "Bill loves meditating because it helps him stay focused and calm."

In *14 Executives Who Swear By Meditation (http://www.businessinsider.com/ceos-who- meditate-2012-5?op=1)*, Business Insider's War Room names these meditating movers and shakers:

- "Hedge fund manager Ray Dalio
- Salesforce.com's Marc Benioff
- Panda Express Founder Andrew Cherng
- Former Monsanto CEO Bob Shapiro
- Former CEO Bill George (Medtronic)
- Def Jam Founder Russell Simmons
- Oprah Winfrey
- Legal Sea Foods CEO Roger Berkowitz
- Green Mountain Coffee Roaster Founder Robert Stiller

- Ramani Ayer, former Chairman and CEO of The Hartford Financial

- Steve Rubin, former CEO and chairman of United Fuels International,

- Executive Management Associates CEO Nancy Slomowitz

- Marnie Abramson, who owns Tower Companies real estate

- Tupperware CEO Rick Goings"

Zimbio.com presents this huge list of *Famous Well Known People who Meditate (http://www.zimbio.com/Meditation/articles/hZ4BatzTWYX/ Famous+Well+Known+People+Meditate)*. Are some of favorites listed here?

- "The Dalai Lama (Religious Leader),

- Albert Einstein (Scientist),

- Mick Jagger (Singer),

- David Lynch (Filmmaker),

- Bruce Lee (Martial Artist),

- Jennifer Lopez (Singer, Actress),

- Clint Eastwood (Actor, Director, Politician),

- Rob Cohen (Director),

- Harrison Ford (Actor),

- George Lucas (Producer),

- Alice Walker (Author),

- Roberto Baggio (Soccer Pro),

- Jerry Seinfeld (Comedian),

- Phil Jackson (NBA Coach),

- Melissa Mathison (Screenwriter),

- Leonard Cohen (Singer, Songwriter, Poet),
- Orlando Bloom (Actor),
- Herbie Hancock (Musician),
- Steven Seagal (Actor),
- Belinda Carlisle (Singer),
- Frank Herbert (Author),
- William Ford Jr. (Ford Motor Company),
- Sting (Singer, Musician),
- Allen Ginsberg (Poet, Author)
- Nathaniel Dorsky (Filmmaker),
- various members of the Beatles (Singers/Musicians),
- K.D. Lang (Singer),
- Andy Kaufman (Actor),
- Cher (Singer, Actress),
- Mark Wahlberg (Actor/Singer)
- Sheryl Crow (Singer, Songwriter),
- Kate Bosworth (Actress)
- Russell Simmons (Record Label Owner),
- Richard Gere (Actor),
- Tiger Woods (Golf Pro),
- Julia Roberts (Actress),
- Gwyneth Paltrow (Actress),
- Tina Turner (Singer),
- Goldie Hawn (Actress),

- Oliver Stone (Movie Producer),

- Elle MacPherson (Supermodel)

- Deepak Chopra (Author),

- Wayne Dyer (Author),

- Paramahansa Yogananda (Guru),

- practically every author and teacher in the spiritual growth a rena,

- native Americans and those who practice shamanism and earth-based spirituality

- yogis and gurus from everywhere"

And finally, in it's Health & Wellbeing page at MSN New Zealand we're presented with this slideshow of *Zen celebs: Famous people who meditate (http://health.msn.co.nz/ slideshow_ajax.aspx?sectionid=75132&sectionname=mind&subsectionid=7806353&*

- "Oprah

- David Lynch

- Russell Brand

- Katy Perry

- Miranda Kerr

- Gemma Ward

- Kristen Bell

- Paul McCartney

- Ellen DeGeneres

- Wes Carr

- Hugh Jackman

- Eva Mendes
- Santigold"

Conclusion

The bottom line: 1) **Meditation provides many scientifically-proven benefits** and is capable of bringing about **tangible, measurable physiological changes.** 2) **Many of the most successful and productive people and organizations rely on it** to help them maintain their successes and overall health.

Where to begin: Many of the articles referenced above include information on how to start your meditation practice. (Just follow the links.) But **you don't need a lot of formal instruction!** Your practice can be as simple as quietly sitting and focusing on your breathing, while witnessing thoughts that arise and gently dismissing them to re-focus on your breathing. That's it! **The key: Be patient and kind to yourself!**

HOW MINDFULNESS MEDITATION HELPS ME LAUGH AT MENTAL SOAP BUBBLES

"Meditation is warm-up exercise for the mind, so that you can jog through the rest of the day without getting agitated or spraining your patience."
— Eknath Easwaran in Conquest of Mind via Brian Johnson's PhilosophersNotes

Mindfulness Meditation & Mental Soap Bubbles

Mindfulness is, in the words of Jon Kabat-Zinn, "paying attention, on purpose, to the present moment, without judgment."

As you are learning to practice mindfulness or meditate mindfully, Kabat-Zinn recommends a "light touch" when you are confronted with stray thoughts that try to distract you. You simply look at these thoughts as they rise up, notice them, and **watch them drift away and pop like soap bubbles.** You might say something like this to yourself: "Oh there it goes. I'm worrying... worrying." Or "There's another. I'm thinking and remembering," and so on. What happens when you apply this "light touch" is that the thoughts just bubble up, drift around, and vanish. You don't engage them in a battle, you don't give them power, and they simply disappear.

As I noted in my podcast Practice Mindfulness (http://www.inspiredprojectteams.com/?p=766), Kabat-Zinn's advice to apply a "light touch" to intruding thoughts and his image of soap bubbles popping is the most useful guidance I ever received regarding meditation. Before I acquired this frame of reference I would waste half my meditation time trying to force myself to concentrate while simultaneously gritting my teeth and battling mental intruders. Instead of bringing peace, my meditation time was a kind of silent warfare.

Here & Now Versus the Bubble Machine

When I try to tell people about this "soap bubble" approach they either wrinkle their brows and look question marks at me or they just roll their eyes and quickly change the subject. If this is your reaction, then I'd like to invite you inside my mindfully-meditating brain to witness a typical interaction between My Here & Now Awareness (MHNA) and that annoying character I call Mental Bubble Machine (MBM). *Let the mindful meditation begin:*

My Here & Now Awareness [MHNA]: Air moving in and out nostrils, nose hairs moving, feel coolness of morning air going across my upper lip. Feeling tranquil. Ahhh...

Mental Bubble Machine [MBM]: "How long have I been meditating? I got work to do. Gotta respond to that email from...."

MHNA [interrupting]: "Worrying... Worrying... We'll do it later, don't worry... Let it go..." Back to noticing air moving in and out, in and out, in and out....

MBM: "Hear that bird song?... Sounds like the mockingbird is back! Must be mating season the way he's singing his heart out. Wow, did you ever notice that when birds mate it only lasts a couple of seconds! Wonder if they wish it would last longer... Wonder if..."

MHNA [interrupting again]: "Really? Birds mating? [laughing] Let it go, dude!" Back to noticing air moving in and out, in and out, in and out....

MBM: "My stomach's growling. I'm hungry! Why don't we ever eat breakfast before we do this?"

MHNA [interrupting again]: "Just a few more minutes and we'll eat. Now take a deep breath... " Back to noticing air moving in and out, in and out, in and out....

MBM: "Hey, I just figured out how to approach that project management article we're trying to write. It's all about using grape jelly as a metaphor for..."

MHNA [interrupting again and reaching for the always-nearby pen and paper]: "OK. Let's capture your insight. See? I'm writing it all down!" [Quickly making notes, then laying down pen & paper, and closing eyes again] Back to noticing air moving in and out, in and out, in and out....

MBM: "Geez. I just remembered the way my Dad used to say that, deep down, I am a lazy guy... always wanted to carry a 'lazy man's load' by trying to move a giant pile of stuff instead of taking the time to carry several smaller, more manageable loads. Can that be right? I don't see how he could say that..."

MHNA [interrupting again]: "Time tripping are we? [laughing] Let it go, dude!" Back to noticing air moving in and out, in and out, in and out....

Helping MHNA and MBM Peacefully Co-Exist

You get the idea. The key here is that MHNA fully expects that MBM is gonna act like a goofy puppy during the mindfulness meditation and run around, make all sorts of noise and generally be annoying. **The key is that MHNA has learned, through frequent interaction, not to take MBM all that seriously.** There is no dramatic battle for control, nor is there panic that control may have been lost.

Better yet, MHNA knows that MBM can be a fun creature to have around — a source of creativity and spontaneity. Witness that idea-worth-noting that bubbled up during the example meditation session above. MBM does this sort of thing for me quite often when I'm trying to mindfully meditate. And I not only appreciate it, I make sure I capture it so I can put that random (but potentially valuable) idea to use after the meditation is over! *(Confession: This article started out as several notes scribbled on a scrap of paper during one of my mindful meditation sessions! Seems MBM was clamoring for attention!)*

At the same time, it's important to remember that most of what MBM serves up is random, useless stuff. And the great thing about witnessing this mental junk and learning to lightly dismiss it is that in the process, I am cultivating a powerful skill that is of great practical value during the non-meditation parts of my life.

For example, when I find myself in a heated discussion with someone and things are getting a bit tense, I often feel the presence of MBM as he starts sending up random resentments from the past and fears of the future that threaten to knock me out of the Here and Now. MBM would very much like me to plug some of this stuff into my discussion and watch the fur fly! But because I've had lots of practice ignoring MBM's nonsense in my morning meditations, it's easier for me to ignore this stuff when he serves it up in my Here and Now. And this makes for much more focused, grown-up discussions and, ultimately, better relationships and more thoughtful decisions.

So You Don't Sprain Your Patience

So back to Eknath Easwaran's quote: **"Meditation is warm-up exercise for the mind, so that you can jog through the rest of the day without getting agitated or spraining your patience."**

How very true! If you spend a little time each morning confronting — and learning to laugh at and dismiss — all that junk that's spit at you by your Mental Bubble Machine, you'll be far less likely to "get agitated or sprain your patience."

Namaste!

———————

(For more info on mindful meditation, check out my free 22 min. podcast Practice Mindfulness – http://www.inspiredprojectteams.com/?p=766.)

LEVERAGING INSPIRATION: 10 SIMPLE PRACTICES TO KEEP YOUR CREATIVE OUTPUT FLOWING

Are you under pressure to produce some sort of creative output? Are you feeling "dried up" or empty? Do you find yourself staring into space and mumbling "I got nothin'!!" ?? Do you wonder how some people seem to be consistently productive while you keep having these "dry spells?" In this article I'm going to share the simple, down-to-earth practices I use to keep the articles, videos and podcasts flowing.

Everyone is Creative... Everyone!

The truth is, everyone is creative. Period. Everyone gets ideas, sees unique connections, has insights, comes up with unusual thoughts. But why do some people seem to produce more creative output than others? The answer is they leverage their creativity. They nurture it. They capture the shimmering bubbles that float into their consciousness before they can pop or drift away. They treat these like the magical gifts that they are and they maximize them by employing some fairly mundane, everyday practices. Here are my favorites:

1. Rain barrels & catch basins: Don't let that idea get away!

One of the ways that home gardeners in semi-arid areas make sure they have enough water for their plants is to capture rain water that runs off their buildings. They carefully position barrels beneath gutters and locate catch basins where the rain water flows. So instead of losing it down the drain, they capture that pure, plant-friendly rain water to use later when there's not enough rain. In a similar way, I position a pad of yellow stickies or note paper outside my shower, near my meditation chair, beside my bed, in the car and in one of my pockets.I also have an app in my phone that takes my dictation in situations where I can't write.

By having all these "catch basins" available, I'm able to snag every little insight, notion, or creative leap that drifts into my consciousness. I can then play with these later and organize them into collections or articles. In fact, I created this article you are now reading by organizing a bunch of these fragments that I had been collecting over the period of a month or so, mostly as phone-recorded dictations! This is probably my most powerful creativity-enhancing practice.

2. Resolve to create a small chunk.

One of the best ways to remove the feeling of overwhelm or "writer's block" is to make this deal with yourself: "I will simply create one small chunk right now. Then I'll come back later and do another chunk." So, if I'm working on a difficult article and feeling a bit intimidated, I might resolve to crack open Evernote and write one single paragraph. I tell myself that if I feel like it, I can always add another — but the goal is to write just one. I simply make that small commitment.

What frequently happens, however, is that when I focus on the ideas for that one little chunk instead of the entire writing chore, momentum begins to build — I slip into the flow of things and the next thing you know a couple of hours have gone by and I've made a ton of progress! And if this doesn't happen, then at least I've added another paragraph to the work. *(**Note**: For this to work properly, you should sequester yourself from all forms of electronic interruptions... shut down everything: all forms of email, text, & social network alerts, your phone... everything!)*

3. Get random! Start in the middle or at the end.

In the beginning of any project, it's okay — sometimes highly desirable — to go wherever the energy takes you. Don't allow a strict focus on an outline or particular structure or exact linearity to bog you down. Start in the middle. Jump to the end. Ramble. Loop. Doodle. Mind map. Plaster a wall with yellow stickies containing idea fragments of all sorts. Don't worry about editing or supporting those raw ideas. Just get them out, get going and do something!

4. In the early stages (first draft, initial concept development, etc.) trust you intuition and don't criticize or second guess yourself.

Think about it. You were excited enough about your idea that you wanted to bring it to life on paper, video, audio, etc. So keep your internal critical voice stifled until you have developed the idea to the point where the work has the strength to stand on its own and be evaluated. And this admonition pertains to anyone you know who tends to be cynical, "realistic" or otherwise a source of negative energy. Avoid them during this stage of your work. When a creative concept of any kind is in the process of being born, it is almost always too fragile to endure any kind of harsh treatment.

So instead of criticizing your new-born creation, flesh it out, nudge it, pick it up, spin it around, play with it, and help it stand on its own. After all, this creation is based on an idea is that bubbled up from somewhere in your intuition, got your attention and motivated you to pursue it. So it deserves to be gently nurtured in its infancy and given a fair chance to grow.

5. Create a little something every day, even if you don't feel like it.

Develop the habit of getting into your "zone of creation" whether you feel like it or not. (See preceding advice about agreeing to create a small chunk.) By insisting on doing a little every day, you develop the strength and discipline to stifle that whiny little voice that presents you with all kinds of excuses to indulge your laziness. You must say to that voice: "I'm gonna try for 15 minutes – – that's all– maybe start in the middle or at the end but at least start playing with the concepts and engage the process. This way I'll at least keep my creative muscles in shape and keep this project from withering away."

6. Lost your "voice?" Find it in another work.

One way to get "unstuck" is to hitch a ride on another creative piece that you've already completed. Ask yourself: What finished article, video, audio, or other creative work seems to have a similar mood or attitude to the one I'm trying to bring to life? Identify it, consume it, and put yourself in the same creative space that produced that work. In this way, you can re-activate that voice and make it sing for you to produce the new creation.

7. Know when to unleash your editor.

Your internal editor is a real buzz killer! He's anal, judgmental, fastidious, fearful of breaking rules, and the kind of entity that can douse the fires of creativity in an instant. So **don't let your internal editor anywhere near your enthusiasm or your creative process.** Get crazy, generate a big pile of creative output, play with it like a bunch of blocks by trying different organizational structures. And ignore any noises that your internal editor is making. Later, when you're finished having fun, you can unleash your editor on your big pile of stuff and he can do what he does best — tidy things up and make them "presentable." (Yep... my internal editor is a "he." That figures, right?)

8. Release it when it's 90% perfect. 90% is just fine!

One of the good things about working with publishers and clients is that they can be ruthless editors. And while their editorial input and demands for revision can be painful to the ego, they can also be liberating. By tearing up my precious work and forcing it to be released with changes that I sometimes didn't like, these folks have taught me a great deal about "perfection." Specifically: **"Perfect" is a fiction. There is no perfect.** There is only "finished"… for now. This is because anyone looking at your work could provide you with some little bit of feedback recommending a change of one kind or another. Anyone! And when you finally make peace with this fact, you realize that there is never any "perfect" form for your work. There is only your version. And pursuing "perfect" can be a productivity killing, time-wasting self-indulgence. **So get it 90% right and release it to the world!** (Then later, simply smile and thank them for their feedback!)

9. Be a curator of your consciousness.

Most art museums have way too many art works to exhibit. They employ a curator to make sensible displays of the works by focusing on one or more themes and organizing them into meaningful collections. This way visitors aren't overwhelmed by a jumble of random stuff. Our consciousness can be like that museum. With our 24-hour cable channels, unlimited info to cruise through on the web, and endless stimuli from circles of electronically connected friends and colleagues, our consciousness can get all jumbled up and stuffed full like a museum basement.

To be a productive creator you need to be a curator your consciousness. Pay attention to where you spend your time and what you bring into your consciousness. When streaming news items or reality TV or online games or a bunch of Tweets or Facebook updates start screaming for your attention, ask yourself: "Is this where I want to spend my time? Is this the world I want to engage? Have I had enough opportunities to simply think? … to quietly 'be here & now' so that my back burner can cook up some new insights and new meaning without having content constantly pouring through and dousing the flame?"

So shut off the radio, close that chat box, turn off the phone, kill that instant alert setting and, yes, meditate. Or go for a walk, run, or bike ride without any electronic input. **Remember: You can't hear your muse if you're not quiet. Silence invites your unique Source of inspiration to speak.**

10. Honor your weirdness.

Reflect on what people are talking about and how you might see things differently. Notice how you might see shades of gray when others see distinctly black and white. Notice how you want to delve a little more deeply into an issue when others are content to form a conclusion quickly. Notice how you see things from odd or unique angles. In particular, pay attention when they tell you that you have just shared a "weird" idea. Honor your weirdness and follow it to new places.

Avoid Creative Malpractice

I truly believe that squandering any of those little bursts of inspiration that are served up to you by your muse is essentially creative malpractice. Remember: **Everyone is creative. The difference between someone who consistently churns out creative output and someone who's "… got nothin'!" is that the former employs a few of these simple, practical methods for leveraging inspiration.**

———————

See my related video *"Time & Space to Blossom"* in my Worth Sharing playlist (https://www.youtube.com/user/greerspm/playlists).

SO WHAT'S YOUR STORY? AND HOW'S IT WORKING FOR YOU?

Stories... narratives... legends... tales of struggles, victories, and losses... we humans spend much of our lives trying to make sense of the world through the lenses of our stories. Whether it recounts events we have lived personally or events lived by others, there is something about a story that is powerfully compelling. And when we finish witnessing or telling or retelling a story, it leaves behind a theme that shapes our feelings about our place in this world and the actions we should take to adapt to it.

The good news: **Stories are powerfully engaging and can help us figure out how to live** our lives more effectively.

The bad news: **Stories are powerfully engaging. And they can trap us inside them** in subtle ways that prevents us from accurately experiencing this moment – this unique here and now. And if we aren't careful, hours and days and years can pass by without our having had direct experience of the truth of this moment because we've been swept up inside all of our stories.

Managing By Story

What's this got to do with project management? It's simple. Your ability to take the right action in a project crisis – i.e., to select the exactly-appropriate, surgically-focused, perfectly-executable action and then "make it so" – depends on your ability to be here, now. You need to see clearly, right now, with this set of project players, with this product, in this unique market environment, with these unique constraints, exactly what is happening. Then, and only then, can you take the most effective action. However, **if you're resonating with a particularly powerful story that is bubbling just below your consciousness when you're trying to decide on your "right action," there's a good chance that your response will be shaped by the story instead of the truth of your "right now."**

Worse yet, because stories are so compelling, it's a lot easier to pay attention... (i.e., to "pay out" of your stash of conscious energy...) to a story than it is to focus on the messy here and now. After all, the story (because it's typically viewed from a distance as a cohesive whole) has a nice, tidy arc to it. It has a beginning, middle, and end. It has clear heroes and villains... clear triumph and loss... clear actions and consequences.

In contrast, the here and now can appear to be a bunch of random events, unfocused characters, and unclear chains of cause and effect. The here and now can be messy and unattractive. So if the here and now is forced to compete with a good story running in your mind, it'll lose every time! The result: Stories pull us in and keep us in their grips while the reality of "here and now" slips by unnoticed.

Think about it: **If you're going to create that next great story – that** next team victory or resounding project success – **you must be able to see this unique moment (this here and now), with all its messy events and characters and indiscernible plot, exactly as it is.** When you see things as they truly are, you will then be able to take the action that will be most effective for this special moment in your project's evolution. And when you do that, you create another great story.

Learn More and Challenge Yourself

In my podcasts Practice Mindfulness and Accept What Is, I shared insights from Jon Kabat-Zinn and others about the advantages of (and techniques for) fully attending to the here and now. Check these out to explore this topic a little more deeply.

In the meantime, **here are three challenges:**

FIRST: Do your own informal "story-time" audit: Specifically, ask yourself these questions:

- How much time do I spend replaying mental movies of stories from the past?

- How much time do I spend inventing and playing mental movies that take place in an imagined future?

- How much time do I spend listening to, encouraging and propagating "war stories?"

- How much time do I spend absorbed in story-bearing media that pulls me out of the "here and now?" (Examples: Gossip via text or Twitter or Facebook or whatever, water cooler gossip, online videos, and so on)

SECOND: Now reflect on the amount of time you spend in stories and **compare this to the amount of time you spend in the here and now.** Are you "in the moment" for your team as often as you might be?

FINALLY: Think about the last tough decision you made.

- To what extent was this decision influenced by a story or theme you liked?

- To what extent was this decision influenced by the unique characteristics of the project itself... it's "here and now?"

The object of the game: Take charge of your stories. Consciously choose to spend time in them and be aware of how they are influencing your world view. Consciously balance the time you spend in stories with the time you spend in the "here and now."

And above all, **when you make an important project decision, make sure it's based on your clear-eyed awareness of reality as it truly is and not based on an inappropriate distortion** as viewed through the lens of your favorite story.

A LESSON FROM THE HUMBLE PELICAN: FIND YOUR UNIQUE MISSION, THEN SOAR!

"A funny old bird is a pelican. His beak can hold more than his belican..." — Dixon Lanier Merritt

I guess I've always had a mild obsession with pelicans. Living a few miles from the ocean and wetlands most of my adult life, I've had the chance to see pelicans in all shapes and sizes — brown and gray and even the occasional white ones.

Once I spot them, I can't take my eyes off them. They soar the updrafts like modern-day pterodactyls, giant wings motionless and outstretched, heads tucked in, long necks disappearing completely. Or they adopt the same glide posture to skim blazingly fast along the water, just inches from the surface, hitch-hiking on an ocean breeze.

Every once in a while they explode out of their not-a-single-muscle-moving form to morph into a dive-bombing fishing machine. I watch in awe as they knife into the water and rocket back to the surface with a live fish flopping around inside that tough, but paper-thin, pouch beneath their beak.

Sleek diving machine… ?

Fish captured (mission accomplished!), they shake the water from their wings, then fold themselves into a clumsy lump of feathers and bob goofily on the waves as their big web feet paddle towards shore.

On land, they waddle-walk like giant ducks with oversized, awkward beak-heads and eventually collapse in the sun, a mass of sleeping feathers.

… or awkward waddler?

So what are these creatures? Are they sleek, dive-bombing fishing machines? Or are they ungainly waddling clowns? It all depends on the context in which you observe them.

They are at their streamlined best when pursuing their noblest mission: stunt flying and fishing. The rest of the time, they are downright clunky, simply hanging out and waiting for the next mission. I can't think of another living thing that so completely transforms itself based on its mission. Except maybe us humans.

So What's Your Mission?

"Everything – a horse, a vine – is created for some duty... For what task, then, were you yourself created? A man's true delight is to do the things he was made for."
– Marcus Aurelius, in The Meditations of Marcus Aurelius

Let's face it. There are things that you are good at — that only you can do and that you do better than anyone else. And when you're doing these things, you can feel your Source or God or whatever creative muse that powers you as it flows through you and brings energy to your work. In short, when you're doing such things, you know you're "in the zone."

The brilliant psychologist Abraham Maslow, who created the term "self-actualization," said: *"Musicians must make music, artists must paint, poets must write if they are to be ultimately at peace with themselves. What human beings can be, they must be. They must be true to their own nature. This need we may call self-actualization."* *(From Maslow's textbook **Motivation and Personality**.)*

So self-actualization — the act of using your unique gifts to become **actually** what you are inherently created to be — is a primal need for all of us. And it must be your highest goal if you are to "be ultimately at peace..."

So what's your unique mission and gift? What excites you... gets you in your zone... makes you lose track of time when your pursue it? As Deepak Chopra says in his **Seven Spiritual Laws of Success**: *"Everyone has a purpose in life... a unique gift or special talent to give to others. And when we blend this unique talent with service to others, we experience the ecstasy and exultation of our own spirit, which is the ultimate goal of goals."*

If you're ever to be at peace with yourself or to find the joy you were created to experience, you must find this purpose. And, once discovered, you need to share it with the world!

The lesson from the humble pelican? You can't spend all day waddling around ignoring and wasting your unique talents. You have to listen to your heart, find your mission and soar!

See also:

- My YouTube video: "Pelicans" (It's in my YouTube Worth Sharing playlist... https://www.youtube.com/user/greerspm/playlists)

CURATE YOUR OWN NEWS: WHY YOU SHOULD AND HOW YOU CAN

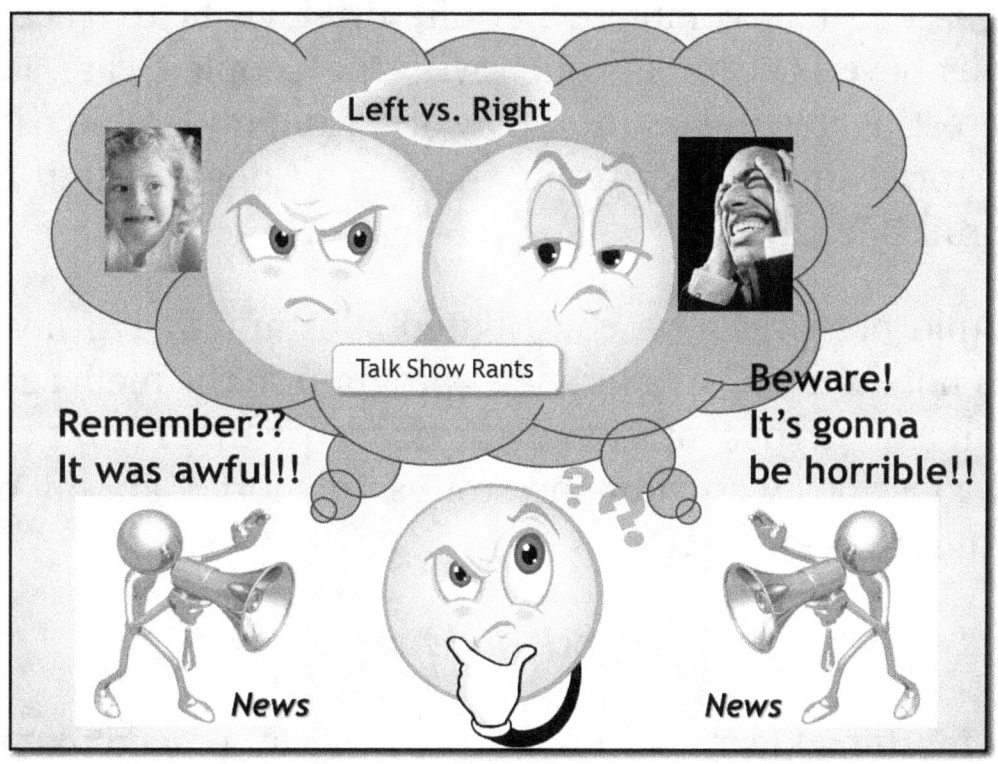

Misery Mongers!

Recently I have been on a news fast. So for the past few months I have been blissfully unaware of what news editors, talk show hosts, entertainment editors, and celebrity-gossipers have decided was important for me to know.

Instead of morning news, I listen to Serius XM's Classical & Spa channels or tech news and business podcasts that I've downloaded to my tablet. And instead of watching the evening news, I've been going for walks and sitting on the porch with my wife, enjoying a couple of beers as the sun goes down. And instead of anything related to serious public affairs (real-life "who-done-its" or probing analysis of the latest scandal, etc.), we've been going straight to Netflix for some light entertainment. I get my weather from a quiet web page that never confronts me with urgent threats and vague promises to give me "details at 11:00!!" So, all-in-all, I am happily ignorant of which famous political figures are hurling insults at their peers.

No. I haven't been a complete hermit. Brief visits to Facebook and Google Plus have kept me in touch with the people I care about. And when interesting news leaks into my world from my online friends, I go after the stories on my own terms through a Google search or a news aggregator like Feedly.

These simple practices have contributed substantially to my peace of mind! I do not "tune in" to a full news program so the media can scream at me about a bunch of sensationalistic nonsense that I don't care about. Instead, I consciously go after the stories. In short, I am my own news curator. And it's been great!

Shock and Awe

The other morning I learned from my online weather feed that there was a huge storm system brewing in the center of the country, so I decided to turn on the TV for the national news and see how this storm might impact my far-flung friends and relatives.

Wow! Was that ever a mistake! After months without screaming headlines, newscasters' warnings of doom and gloom and scandal-driven celebrity gossip, I had completely forgotten how jarring and downright disturbing this stuff could be. In just a few minutes' time I was slammed with gory details about a journalist's beheading, rumors of new terrorist threats, the further spread of the Ebola epidemic and some nonsense about a famous sports figure who was caught up in a sex scandal. I could feel my blood pressure rising — and my peace of mind evaporating — as this stuff washed over me. After about 10 minutes of this drek, I deciding that waiting for their summary of weather developments just wasn't going to be worth the negative crap I'd have to wade through.

Now here's the thing: Because I had spent months without it, I had completely forgotten how intensely disturbing this junk could be. Worse, **there was nothing I could do about any of it! There was absolutely nothing actionable*!** And in the case of the sports figure's sex scandal, I simply felt like a peeping Tom staring in this guy's bedroom window. This was just none of my business! And the talking heads that disingenuously pretended to explain this stuff through their "analysis" were just adding their own half-baked speculation, "what if" hand-wringing and "witch hunt" rants to the mix.

The result: These few minutes of abrasive national news, after a blissful couple of months without it, convinced me that my home-made, tech-driven process of sifting and sorting my own news was the only way to go!

News Curation: Taking Charge of Your Own News Stream

When you visit a collection in a museum or library or art gallery, there is usually a theme that ties the items in the collection together. The curator has carefully chosen objects that support a theme. Instead of simply dumping hundreds of items onto the display floor, the curator consciously selects, sequences, labels and organizes them.

Similarly, you can think of yourself as the curator of your own news. Instead of letting all the media outlets bury you in random stories, you can use tools like Feedly, Pocket, Netvibes, Zinio, TuneIn Radio, etc. to pick and choose the news sources and news stories that you want to know more about. (More on the mechanics of this in the video below.)

These tools will let you apply your own criteria, based on what you personally value, to sort through the days "news" and control what invades your consciousness. For example, here are some questions I ask myself when I am trying to decide whether a news source or particular article/video is worth my time:

- Is this content stream coming at me uninvited or am I inviting it in?

- After two minutes in this stream do I feel better or worse?

- Does this stream enhance my peace of mind and sense of well being? (If not, why I am I exposing myself to it?)

- Is there something actionable* here? (Can I DO something about it? Or is it simply peeping Tom gossip or fear-mongering sensationalism?)

- *(And when I get headlines from an agitated friend breathlessly bearing news, I say:)* "No, I haven't heard that. Explain it go me. What does it mean to you?" *(Then I add it to my list to be curated & researched if I'm really interested.)*

Check out my YouTube video "Curate Your Own News: Why & How." It illustrates why you should curate your own news and describes some specific tech tools that can help you do so. It could help you reclaim your peace of mind! *Enjoy.*

––––––––––––

** Some Thoughts on "Actionable" News*

By "actionable news" I mean any news stories that can lead you to get out of your chair and take a specific action of some sort. It's important to distinguish this kind of news from the gossip and sensationalism — the kind of stuff that captures your attention (like a 75-car pile up on a freeway) — that you simply can't do anything about.

So let's say you learn about a terrible, but legal, injustice that has been inflicted upon someone and it really stirs you up emotionally. This is a potentially "actionable" news story. Here are some positive, productive actions you might take:

- **Do some research and become informed** about the laws related to this story so you can figure out how you might help.

- **Get involved with an advocacy group** that helps victims of such laws.

- **Get involved with a political action committee** who is trying to change such laws.

- **Become an activist** and write letters, call lawmakers, demonstrate, etc.

In contrast, here are some useless, negative actions in response to the story:

- **Tune in to TV or radio talk shows** that rant, inflame and otherwise exploit the story and allow you to relive the feelings again and again.

- **Spend time digging up overly-opinionated blog posts,** podcasts, etc. that also exploit the story.

- **Rehash the story with all your friends** so they can experience (over and over and over!) all the negative feelings you have about the story.

- **Tweet or make Facebook posts that complain and rant and blame**, but that do not advocate a single, specific positive action that can make things better.

Can you feel the difference in the two kinds of responses? So here's the deal: **News stories — especially "actionable" news stories — can help make the world a better place if you use them as a springboard for positive action. It's up to you,** as curator of your personal news feed and the master of your own actions, to figure out how to alchemize these stories and the emotions they generate into a better world!

ARE YOU CLINGING TO YOUR MUMMIFIED PAST?

Gana clinging to her loss

The poignant images above were posted at Flickr by lunlun16. They were part of a story about Gana, a gorilla at the zoo in Munster, Germany and her response to the death of her 3-month old son. Gana simply wouldn't let go. She wouldn't let anyone near the lifeless corpse. These images got me thinking about how we sometimes hold on to our past tragedies, pains, and suffering long after it's time to let go.

My Friend's Self-Inflicted Wounds

Shortly after learning about Gana, I found myself listening to a guy I've known for years go on and on (for the umpteenth time!) about something that had caused him great pain. His story tells how several decades ago he had been badly mistreated by someone close to him. And despite years of outrage, anger, resentment, and demands that he deserved an apology, he never received one. Though the abuser is long gone and out of his life, this event continues to poison him. It colors his self image. And it shapes his interactions with others. But despite the pain, he won't let it go. He keeps it alive by the animated telling and retelling of the story. I've heard it many times.

But this time as I listened to him, the images of Gana were fresh in my mind. Like Gana, this man was holding on to something that had been an important part of his past. Like Gana, he refused to let go. And, like Gana, he caused those who witnessed his clinging to become simultaneously horrified and filled with compassion. Though an outside observer can quickly see the futility of carrying a mummified corpse from the past, both Gana and my friend somehow seemed to derive meaning from it. In some perverse way they had defined themselves by their ugly burdens.

Mummies Are Bad for Your Health!

Now I'm no psychologist. So I can't speculate about what deep psychic motives might provoke someone to cling to tragedy. But as one who's been on the receiving end of these stories, I can tell you that they've made it difficult for me to deal with this guy. Unless I'm feeling extraordinarily energetic and positive, I avoid him. Who wants to feel sad? … or angry? … or helpless because you can't travel back in time and protect this guy from something that happened so long ago? So I find that with repeated exposures to his story my compassion is fading and my impatience is increasing. He seems absolutely determined to make me watch this mental movie of his over and over and over again. Worse, he seems to have resolved that it will be a defining moment in his life's narrative.

It reminds me of the poem "In the Desert" by Stephen Crane:

In the desert
I saw a creature, naked, bestial,
Who, squatting upon the ground,

Held his heart in his hands,
And ate of it.

I said, "Is it good, friend?"
"It is bitter—bitter," he answered;
"But I like it
"Because it is bitter,
"And because it is my heart."

Long ago, as a sophomore English Literature student and innocent moth-drawn-to-the-flame newcomer to the bleakness of Existentialism, I found Crane's poem strangely compelling — even ennobling in its proof that life was pain that must be somehow embraced. However, today, as a guy with lots of miles on my psyche, I find Crane's poem and it's perspective to be darkly self-indulgent.

Let It Go, Already!

Decades of adult life have shown me that everyone eventually faces tragedy of one kind or another. Everyone must endure pain. But everyone need not add the overlay of endless self-inflicted suffering by replaying memories that rekindle the fires of their pain again and again. Researchers tell us that the retelling of any life-story almost guarantees that it be assigned larger amounts of brain real estate (i.e., more neurons) so it may be more easily called up and vividly remembered. Worse, since our ever-vigilant "fight or flight" response system can't seem to tell the difference between tragedy that is remembered versus tragedy that is actually happening in the here and now, it's just not healthy to relive miseries from the past! In order to survive and thrive, we can't afford much backward gazing at tragedy. As Chuck Palahniuk says (my bold added):

"When you understand that **what you're telling is just a story. It isn't happening anymore.** When you realize the story you're telling is **just**

words, when **you can just crumble it up and throw your past in the trashcan**, then we'll figure out who you're going to be."

So are you clinging to mummified corpses from your past? Isn't it time to move on and destroy their power over your future?

———————

(For more info on getting your mind right, check out these podcasts [http://www.inspiredprojectteams.com/?page_id=819]:

- *Consciously Choose Your Attitude*
- *Learn to Be Optimistic... Learn to Succeed*
- *Take Charge... Stop Playing the Victim)*

PALM TREES AND PEAR BLOSSOMS OR 10 FEET OF DOG POOH? IT'S A CHOICE!

Below is a photo of one of my favorite places — the neighborhood walking path/bike trail I use for morning exercise and evening strolls. Stately palm, decorative pear, and fragrant eucalyptus trees border the path, along with several types of flowering shrubs and drought-tolerant ground cover.

Not long ago this beautiful urban retreat was an ugly, abandoned railroad right-of-way. A narrow, dusty strip of coastal desert, it collected broken-down couches & mattresses, wind-blown plastic bags and other trash. Its transformation into a several-miles-long strip of park is something we're all grateful for. Not only has it improved the visual landscape of our neighborhood, it's also encouraged lots of people to walk, bike, jog, or simply get out of the house for an hour or two every day and enjoy the balmy California weather.

Now, I've become a bit protective of this area. And while it's not exactly an untouched wilderness, it still manages to provide enough of Nature's Green to rejuvenate us city folks. So when I come across candy wrappers or potato chip bags thoughtlessly abandoned, I pick them up and take them to a trash can. This only adds a few seconds to my walk, yet it returns the path to an uncluttered state that helps conceal the fact that hundreds of people use it daily.

But What About the Dog Pooh?

The other morning, just as I was beginning my power walk, I came across a nasty trail of dog pooh. It looked like five or six big dogs and their owners had decided that the walkway was a perfect place to rid themselves of their solid waste. So there it was. A long line of this unsightly stuff lay scattered along 10 or 12 feet of bright green, freshly-mowed grass. Not having a plastic bag or other hand-protecting collection tool, I couldn't do anything about this smelly mess. And even if I had the tools, I was due back at my desk for an online meeting soon, so I really had to keep moving. I pushed on, swinging my weights and striding faster to reach my cardio-aerobic zone.

"Why, I Oughta…"

Unfortunately, as I continued to walk that dog pooh walked with me. Angry questions started bubbling up. Who did these dog owners think they were? Did they expect everyone to endure their dogs' waste? How irresponsible can you be? Are the rest of us just supposed to ignore this? What if I confronted one of them or caught one in the act of "pooh and run?" … Maybe I could flag down a police cruiser and tell them what was up!

As I walked, I twice passed someone with a dog and each time found myself staring hard at them, looking for their plastic pick-up bag.

"C'mon, you…" I said to myself, my heart pumping with cardio energy and (just a touch, maybe) anger, "… just try to walk away from you dog's mess and you'll have to deal with me!" I told myself I had to take a stand! On behalf of everyone else who'll be walking here I need to put a stop to this!

Suddenly — out of nowhere it seemed — it appeared. I was at my turn-around point. I thought, "Wow… that was fast! What happened to the first half of my walk?" I did an "about face" and began striding toward home.

I soon came upon that old guy with a white beard who always says "Hi." I dimly remembered walking past him a few minutes ago, but had to admit I didn't acknowledge him. This time I nodded and smiled and he beamed back that toothy bright smile of his. Up ahead, a squirrel was being chased around a palm trunk by a crow. Both creatures yelled at each other in their own critter-specific voices. Passing a pear tree, I marveled at the pink blossoms and how they seemed to be designer-picked to color coordinate with the dark maroon leaves that framed them.

As I passed a shrub, a bunch of yellow vining ground flowers appeared, punctuating the green expanse of grass along the sandy path.

The morning sun spotlighted a couple of these flowers and they appeared to glow. It occurred to me that there was a lot of great stuff to see out here this morning — and friendly people to greet along the way. A wave of gratitude swept over me and I was truly glad to be here. So why hadn't I seen all this on the first half of my walk?

By Pooh Obsessed

The answer, of course, was the dog pooh! I had allowed that stuff to pollute my entire outbound walk. It had effectively blinded me from seeing all the rest of the goodness that was around me. And the sad truth is, the offending droppings were restricted to a 10 – 12 foot long strip of grass. 10 to 12 feet! Now, at my height (6′ 3″ tall) I have a stride of about 3 feet. So in three or four strides, I was past this nasty mess. The rest of my walk involved a mile or two of unspoiled pathway with interesting sights and people to engage. But my ranting brain managed to screen it all out, obsessed by a tiny pile of nasty stuff and a fantasy-war against the phantom dog-owners who might be the source of more nasty.

Well, There's a Half Hour I'll Never Get Back!

The lesson here: It's my choice… my consciousness… my awareness. And I can point this awareness at dog pooh or I can point it at palm trees & pear blossoms & squirrels & flowers & smiling old guys. It's up to me. Ultimately, I have to decide where I want to live. Do I want to inhabit an angry war zone ("Damn those thoughtless dog owners!") or a crisp, sunny morning with life and energy all around me?

Finding & Solving Problems: A Way of Life?

So how's all this relate to project teams and project managers? Here's the deal: Good project managers inevitably develop a kind of finely-tuned radar that continually seeks out problems to be engaged and eliminated. And if you're not careful, this radar will keep whirling and beeping and eventually blind you to the quiet successes… the small victories… the beautiful creations that your team achieves. Instead of seeing anything worth celebrating, you can only see defects, large and small.

So ask yourself: Am I sometimes stepping back from all the problems on my project and allowing myself to see the good stuff that's happening? And when I see the good stuff, do I shine a light on it so the rest of the team can enjoy it or be proud of it?

After all, this is your life that's going by. And the quality of this life derives from your consciousness... what you are aware of... where you "live" inside that big ol' problem-solving brain of yours. So take the time to step back, take a break from finding and dealing with all that pooh and see and celebrate the good stuff.

———————

(See also this podcast: Let Go Perfectionism [http://www.inspiredprojectteams.com/?p=276].)

HURRICANE SANDY: SHINING A LIGHT ON SURRENDER, ACCEPTANCE AND FOCUSED ACTION

Hurricane Sandy's coastal devastation

Nothing clarifies thoughts and actions like a life-and-death situation. As I write this, Hurricane Sandy has smashed into the Eastern U.S. and is at this moment churning its way through millions of lives. And today the media is filled with stories of first responders and ordinary citizens pulling together, focusing their energies and fighting to save lives and property.

Everyone is acting on this unspoken premise: **Now is not the time for hand-wringing, complaining, or agonizing over "Why here?... Why**

now? Why us?" Instead, it's a time to take action to save lives and prevent as much injury and damage as possible.

Hurricane Sandy, for all its horrific destruction, is shining a light on the amazing power of non-resistance to achieve appropriate results. Determined to survive, people in the storm's path quickly move through **surrender** *(Resistance is, after all, truly futile!)* to **acceptance** *(OK. We can't change this. It's happening. It is what it is.)* to **focused action** *(What's the next, most important action... and the next... and the next?).* The result: Lives are saved, property damage is mitigated, and a return path to normalcy is quickly charted.

Everyone on the scene realizes that to deny the reality of the situation, to bemoan past issues, or to wistfully imagine an alternate future makes no sense in this emergency! They intuitively realize that to allow themselves to get tangled up in denial, or agonize over what might have been or what ought to be, simply wastes time and drains away energy that could be used to solve immediate, life-or-death problems.

Deepak Chopra, in *The Seven Spiritual Laws of Success*, describes how important it is to accept what is and not get caught up fighting against reality: "This means that your acceptance of this moment is total and complete. You accept things as they are, not as you wish they were in this moment. This is important to understand. You can wish for things in the future to be different, but in this moment you have to accept things as they are." His point: **to make clear-eyed, effective decisions about this moment you simply can't struggle against reality and waste energy wishing things weren't so.** Only then will you make the best choices and have the strength to carry out these choices.

Of course this hurricane is a terrible tragedy. But, at the same time, it's an opportunity to remind ourselves of the latent wisdom within us all that can propel ordinary folks to become local heroes who are able to dispense with their angst, quickly accept what is, and get on with the right course of action.

We would all do well to listen with our hearts as the media present us with examples of survivors and first responders who push back against Hurricane Sandy's destruction. And we should ask ourselves, "What can I learn from them about surrender, acceptance, and focused action?"

---

* Photo by **Creative Commons/mike609** via **ATVN** (Annenberg TV News), USC/Annenberg School for Communication & Journalism, http://www.atvn.org/news/2012/10/hurricane-sandy-strikes-close-home

---

*(See also this podcast: **Accept What Is** – http://www.inspiredprojectteams.com/?p=752.)*

EVERYTHING YOU OWN, OWNS YOU BACK! (SO ACQUIRE WITH CARE!)

A modern-day Gulliver, strapped down by his belongings

Recently we sold a summer home that we had owned for more than 20 years. Located in rural northwestern Pennsylvania, where we grew up, it provided us with a yearly change of scenery and the opportunity to reconnect with old friends and family. The place was great for holding cook-outs and bonfires or just hanging out and watching birds, rabbits and deer cross the yard on their way to the hardwood forest out back.

After a few years this double-home lifestyle began to take an increasingly larger toll on our peace of mind. In the winter, while we were safe and warm in California, we worried about pipes bursting in the empty Pennsylvania house as temperatures plunged below zero and stayed there for days at a time. And spring thunderstorms (often accompanied by hail or even tornadoes) posed their own threats to the place. To make sure everything was okay during these weather outbreaks we would have to ask relatives or a neighbor to brave the elements and check on the place.

And then there was that large, green lawn. Unless we returned very early in Spring, we'd have to make arrangements for it to be mowed and tended by those same volunteers. Eventually, of course, we'd arrive and whip that big yard into shape. But this typically took the better part of a full day every week we were there.

Over the years, our time in PA was increasingly spent on additional maintenance chores. The water from the well was brought into the house by a submersible pump that had to be repaired and eventually replaced. And the iron-saturated water, a legacy of ground-water contamination by local coal strip mining during the 1950s, had to be treated with strong chemicals in order to be usable. These chemicals, in turn, would become saturated themselves with iron, requiring monitoring. If you waited too long to replace them, you might find that your laundry, instead of becoming clean, had acquired a deep red-brown permanent stain.

Eventually an ancient natural gas well that supplied the house with gas for heating and cooking simply ran out of gas. So we had to arrange for the local gas company to install a brand new gas line to the place. (It had never had a "gas company" gas line!) What's more, those torrential rains that kept those beautiful hills green finally resulted in leaks in the roof and foundation that had to be repaired by specialists. And there were many other chores large and small that our ownership of the place had earned us.

After a few years of this split-home-base lifestyle, we started to realize that we were living in constant home maintenance mode, no matter where we were. Since each house stood exposed to the elements all year long, each gradually developed issues that had to be urgently attended to during our part-time stays there. (We typically spent about 6 months in each place, while the other, empty place simply stood there baking in the sun or hunkered down in the wet or frozen precipitation.)

Everything You Own Owns You Back!

One day, as I was shopping for the supplies for still another home maintenance chore, I began to feel particularly weary of this maintenance-intense lifestyle. In fact, I felt downright claustrophobic! Trapped by all the stuff I owned! It was at that moment that I heard these words bubble up through my consciousness: *"Everything you own, owns you back!"*

WOW!! What an epiphany! I shook my head in disgust and mumbled, "You can say that again, brother!" Every thing I owned was revealing its own maintenance demands. Everything — all those plumbing fixtures and walls and ceilings and heating units and roof shingles and rain gutters and electronics and appliances and gas lines and electric lines and landscaping elements — even the tools to do the fixing– all this stuff was consuming me with maintenance demands! *Everything I owned absolutely owned me back!*

I felt like Gulliver on the beach in Lilliput. But instead of Lilliputians staking me to the sand, I was crushed by all these things, each with its little rope attached to me, nailing down my psyche and my time and my effort.

It was then that I experienced a huge shift in my consciousness. I could no longer count these things among my blessings. Instead, they had all become burdens. Discussing this with my wife, I discovered that she was feeling the same way. And before long we sold that second home in the country and experienced our first California winter in more than two decades absolutely free from the worry of freezing pipes back East.

And this was followed by a CA spring and summer that were free of the fear of Eastern thunderstorms and tornadoes and undone maintenance chores. *We were free!*

The Lesson Learned: Acquire with Care!

Two decades of split-home living taught me a lesson I now know deep in my bones: I absolutely must be conscious of everything I acquire, as I acquire it, since everything has the potential to extend its tentacles deep into my peace of mind and suck the life out of my life!

Think about it: If you're a responsible adult, you honor your commitments whether they are to simply maintain the stuff you own or follow through with a new process you've just set up and agreed to use. Some examples: You have a car, you take it in for maintenance, check the oil regularly, make sure you have enough gas to get where you need to go. You have a lawn, you mow it, edge it, maybe even weed it once in a while. You have a dog, you walk it and pick up its waste. You tell your team you'll do weekly project status reports, you do your best to prepare and distribute them, even when you don't feel like it. You commit to a Project Post Mortem, you take the time to organize it and execute it and prepare that Lessons Learned report, even though everyone is thoroughly sick of the project and just wants to move on!

The point is that **responsible adults feel the pull of commitment from everything they own, everyone they agree to serve and every process or tool they agree to use.** All these things acquire "mind share" and a certain amount of effort in maintenance. In short, **the relationship with any acquisition is reciprocal! It may give you something, but *you* will be giving something in return**, even if it's just a little of your peace of mind.

So the next time you are about to buy something or commit to use a new process or develop a new business relationship with someone, step back and **ask these four questions:**

1. What is the purpose of this?
2. How much effort will it take to maintain?
3. Is this worthwhile? (Will there be a large enough return?)
4. How much energy will this pull from my creativity, my peace of mind, my family and the quality of my other efforts?

Think carefully about your answers to these questions.

Then commit to your acquisition cautiously. After all, **ultimately everything you own owns you back!**

PM LEADERSHIP AND VISION

This Part examines the broader organizational context of PM (project management) and suggests ways that would-be PM leaders might clarify their PM vision and create a better organizational climate for PM.

WHAT'S PROJECT PORTFOLIO MANAGEMENT (PPM) AND WHY SHOULD PROJECT MANAGERS CARE ABOUT IT?

What Is Project Portfolio Management (PPM)?

Project Portfolio Management (PPM) is a management process designed to help an organization acquire and view information about all of its projects, then sort and prioritize each project according to certain criteria, such as strategic value, impact on resources, cost and so on. The objectives of PPM are similar to the objectives of managing a financial portfolio: 1) To become conscious of all the individual listings in the portfolio 2) To develop a "big picture" view and a deeper understanding of the collection as a whole. 3) To allow sensible sorting, adding, and removing of items from the collection based on their costs, benefits, and alignment with long-term strategies or goals. 4) To allow the portfolio owner to get the "best bang for the buck" from resources invested.

Typically, PPM begins with the organization developing an inventory (i.e., a comprehensive list) of all its projects and enough descriptive information about each to allow them to be analyzed and compared. Such descriptive info can include project name, estimated duration, estimated cost, business objective, how the project supports the organization's overall strategies, and so on. These are sometimes compiled in a database using resource management software so they may be analyzed and compared more easily.

After the project inventory is created, the PPM process requires department heads or other unit leaders to examine each project and prioritize it according to established criteria. *(More on this later in "Too Many Projects? Prioritize Them!")* The overall list of projects is then considered in order to develop a well-balanced list of supported projects. Some projects will be given high priority and extensive support, some will be given moderate priority, and still others will be placed on hold or dropped entirely from the list.

Finally, the project portfolio is reevaluated by the portfolio management team on a regular basis (monthly, quarterly, etc.) to determine which projects are meeting their goals, which may need more support, or which may need to be down-sized or dropped entirely. Since the circumstances of each project and the business environment can change rapidly, PPM is most effective when the portfolio is frequently revisited and actively managed by the team.

In order for the above PPM activities to take place, the organization must first decide who will participate as active managers of the PPM process. Typically, the PPM management team is made up of department heads from sub-organizations which generate requests for projects, provide project resources (especially team members), provide project funding, use finished project deliverables, set strategic directions, and so on. After the PPM management team is established, they must agree on a set of criteria for valuing projects in order to prioritize them. Decisions based on these criteria will likely be more acceptable to everyone in the organization if the criteria have been developed with the input or review of as many stakeholders as possible from within the various sub-organizations. So typically broad, organization-wide discussions of the criteria are held before they are finalized.

Why Should Project Managers Care about PPM?

Project managers who find themselves continually frustrated by lack of resources or by other organizations stealing their resources should be especially interested in PPM. These frustrations are symptoms of an unbalanced (or unacknowledged) project portfolio. In short, the frequent complaint of "not enough resources," is simply another way of saying that there are too many projects! And if there are too many projects, then someone should be sorting them out, prioritizing them, and "killing" the projects that aren't high priority.

Every project manager wants to have enough resources available to complete high-quality project deliverables, on-time and within budget. And every project manager wants to work on projects that are perceived to be valuable and, therefore, enjoy plenty of support throughout the organization. PPM can help project managers achieve both of these visions.

What Should Project Managers Do about PPM if None Exists in Their Organizations?

The average project manager is not in a position to implement PPM alone. Meaningful PPM cannot exist without the support and active involvement of managers at the highest levels of the organization. But these senior managers are not likely to initiate PPM unless they are aware there is a documented need for it. So if you believe your organization could benefit by PPM, you need to first educate yourself, then build your case for PPM, and, finally, present this case to your senior managers. Here are *some specific steps* you might take:

1. Look for symptoms that PPM is needed and document them. Typical symptoms include:

- Frequent difficulty finding enough people to put together a solid project team

- Excessive project delays due to "not enough resources"

- High turnover due to "burn out" of key project contributors because they are working on too many projects and spending too many overtime hours

- Frequent change of status of projects (i.e., moving from "active" to "on hold" to "top priority" and back)

- Completion of projects that, when all is said and done, don't really meet a strategic need

- Intense competition, rather than cooperation, among departments and sub-organizations when staffing and funding projects

2. Learn more about PPM. You might:

- Talk to other professionals in your field and see how PPM is being applied in their companies.

- Search the internet and find out more about PPM. There are plenty of good articles and YouTube videos available that can take you deeper into PPM theory and issues.

3. Document your resource requirements and share these with your senior management. Specifically:

- Create "high resolution" project plans that accurately spell out, in vivid detail, the resources required to complete each task and activity

- Capture the actual hours spent by all project players in completing project tasks and activities

- Create summary tables showing planned and actual time spent by each person in your organization on every project to which he or she is assigned in order to demonstrate who's overloaded

- Document all incidents of resources that are "stolen" across projects, excessive overtime, large-effort-but-ultimately-useless projects, and so on.

- By conducting project "post mortem" evaluations, gather information about how systematic PPM might have prevented problems and encouraged successes. *(See "Project 'Post Mortem' Review Questions for more.)*

4. **Make your case for establishing PPM** in your organization.

Conclusion

Effective PPM can help make a project manager's life much easier and more professionally rewarding. More importantly, it can help an organization align its project workload to meet its strategic goals, while making the best use of limited resources. But PPM can't be effective without solid, well-documented project plans, accurate estimates of resource requirements, and accurate information about actual resources consumed. Project managers who are equipped with such high resolution project artifacts are in a good position to start a grass roots movement to sell PPM and help senior managers decide how to set up the best PPM system for their organizations. What's more, once the PPM is up and running, it is these same high resolution artifacts that provide the accuracy necessary for good decision-making by the PPM team.

(Disclaimer: I do not claim expertise in establishing or maintaining PPM systems. There are plenty of vendors who can help with this and provide sophisticated software to support PPM decision-making. I do, however, have substantial experience helping project managers develop the planning and tracking skills to achieve the high resolution project artifacts necessary to support PPM. See The Project Management Minimalist, The Project Manager's Partner or visit my website for my recommended tools. –M.G.)

GO TOO MANY PROJECTS? PRIORITIZE THEM!

Too Many Projects

Does your organization have more projects than it can handle? It's easy for smart, creative people to generate lots of good ideas for projects. And soon, if you're not careful, you can easily have more projects going than you have people, time, and money to complete them. When your list of pending projects becomes overwhelming, you've got to figure out how to sort through them and prioritize them. But how do you separate the high priority projects from those that are less important? The answer: You need to develop some sort of objective prioritization criteria, then apply these to your list of pending projects.

Prioritize Your Projects

In my PM classes and consulting, I've worked with many organizations to help them develop a customized approach, based on their unique organization's values, to compare projects and prioritize them. Then, after their projects are prioritized, the organization can fund and support the higher-priority projects, leaving the lower-priority projects to be completed later, when more resources are available.

Note: It's particularly important that project prioritization criteria be locally-developed, since these should reflect your organization's unique strategic directions, values, and business priorities. While I can't help you figure out what's important to your organization, I can share with you a generic approach that can be a springboard for developing your own, custom-tailored prioritization scheme.

A Generic Approach to Prioritizing Projects

Here's a simple, generic, 3-step approach to prioritizing your project list:

1. **Determine your criteria and create a ranking scale** for discriminating among projects. For example:

- *Strategic Value:* Is it important to our organization's overall strategies? [1 = Highly important 5 = Not important]

- *Ease:* Will this project be fairly easy to complete? [1 = Very easy 5 = Very difficult]

- *Financial Benefit:* Will the project's deliverables likely yield financial benefit? [1 = Highly likely 5 = Not likely]

- *Cost:* Will this project likely cost a lot? [1 = Low cost 5 = High cost]

- *Resource Impact:* Will this project have a great impact on our resources (people, equipment, etc.)? [1 = Low impact 5 = High impact]

NOTE: You can, of course, add and change criteria. You can also weight certain criteria to give them more value in the overall score. Be creative! It's your organization, your values, and your prioritization scheme!

2. **Make a grid or table** with the **names of your prioritization criteria** across the top and the **names of potential projects** down the left column.
3. **Review each project and apply a value (based on the ranking scale) for each of the criteria. Then add up the total scores for each project, divide them by the number of criteria and determine their priority.** This step might be completed in two stages: First, individually, by managers or supervisors from various organizations that provide resources (people, facilities, equipment,

and money) to projects. Second, as a group effort with these managers and supervisors getting together to compare notes on their prioritization results to develop a master list of prioritized projects that everyone agrees on.

Below is an example of a completed project prioritization worksheet:*

Sample
Project Prioritization Worksheet

Project	Strategic Value	Ease	Financial Benefit	Cost	Resource Impact	Overall Priority	Notes
Project A [name]	1	3	3	5	2	2.8	
Project B [name]	5	2	4	4	4	3.8	
Project C [name]	3	5	3	3	5	3.8	
Project D [name]	2	4	3	3	5	3.4	
Project E [name]	5	3	5	3	2	3.6	
Project F [name]	1	2	2	5	4	2.4	
Project G [name]	1	2	1	2	2	1.6	

Priority ratings (your best guess or judgments) should be scored as follows:

Strategic Value? Is the project important to our overall strategies? (1 = Highly important 5 = Not important)

Ease? Will this project be fairly easy to complete? (1 = Very easy 5 = Very difficult)

Financial Benefit? Will the project's deliverables likely yield financial benefit? (1 = Highly likely 5 = Not likely)

Cost? Will this project likely cost a lot? (1 = Low cost 5 = High cost)

Resource Impact? Will this project have a great impact on our resources (people, equipment, etc.)? (1 = Low impact 5 = High impact)

Overall Priority: Average score, all five criteria.

NOTE: The *lower* the score, the *higher* the project's priority.

A sample Project Prioritization Worksheet

Conclusion

In broad terms, this entire process of prioritizing projects is typically conducted across functional lines, often by the heads of the organization's various departments or their designees. Taken together, these people sometimes develop a working team referred to as the "project office" who meet regularly to try to manage the overall collection of active and pending projects as a "project portfolio."

---

* *Note:* **You can make a similar worksheet to prioritize your personal project list** or your **family project list.** For example, one of my PM students used it to help prioritize a long list of small remodeling projects which she and her husband were contemplating. By prioritizing them, she was able to make certain that the most important projects would be completed first – before they ran out of money!

BE A ROLE MODEL OF PM MINIMALISM: MANAGE YOUR PROJECTS WITH A 1-PAGE CHECKLIST!

Are you ready to cut through all the usual PM garbage and "go Minimalist?" *OK!*

Step 1: Get the PM Minimalist Quick Start Guide.

The PM Minimalist Quick Start Guide is designed to help you plan and manage your first project using the PM Minimalist approach. The **38-page Quick Start Guide** includes:

- *Project Management Minimalist Quick Start Checklist* — You can use this simple tool to plan and manage an entire project.

- *Quick Start Post Mortem Worksheet: Audit, Adjust, & Keep It Simple!* — You can use this tool to conduct a "post mortem" of any project and discover some "lessons learned" so you can do better next time.

- *PM Minimalist Values Checklist* — A one-page list of the 10 values that can help you think like a "PM Minimalist"

- *PM Minimalist Values Explained* — Full explanations and examples of each of the 10 PM Minimalist Values

- *Learn More* — Live ("hot") links to online articles, downloadable documents, and audio/video media that provide practical advice for applying PM Minimalism *(Note: If your reader is Wi-Fi enabled, you could go directly to these links from the Quick Start Guide while you're reading it.)*

Click one of the links below to start your free download – or get 'em all, if you want to!
(All are available here: http://michaelgreer.biz/?p=3684)

- MOBI version: Click here to download the "mobi" version for your Kindle or other mobi-based device.

- EPUB version: Click here to download the "epub" version for your NOOK, iPad, or other epub-based device. *(Apple iPad users: After you've downloaded this file to your computer, please see How To Add Epub Books To Your iPad Without iTunes [iOS Tips] for detailed info about loading the file onto your Apple device.)*

- PDF version: Click here to download the PDF version — (*Note*: PDF is the best choice if you intend to print hard copies of the pages on paper. It uses a fixed format, instead of the "flowing" text format of the epub & mobi files.)

Step 2: Use the Quick Start Checklist to plan & manage a project.

(The one-page Quick Start Checklist)

Step 3: Step back and think...

After you've used the *Quick Start Checklist* to plan or manage your first PM Minimalist-style project, then step back and **think about this cosmic question:**

- What do I need to change (what PM processes, artifacts, etc.) do I need to add or subtract to improve my PM without overloading it with PM administrivia?

Step 4: Download the PDF of the flowchart shown here & make some decisions.

- Use the chart to help you decide what you need to change for your next project. (The **PDF includes lots of links to references** you can consult, if needed.)

- REPEAT this process frequently to refine your project management practices, "strip out" all the excess administrivia and become a *Project Management Minimalist!*

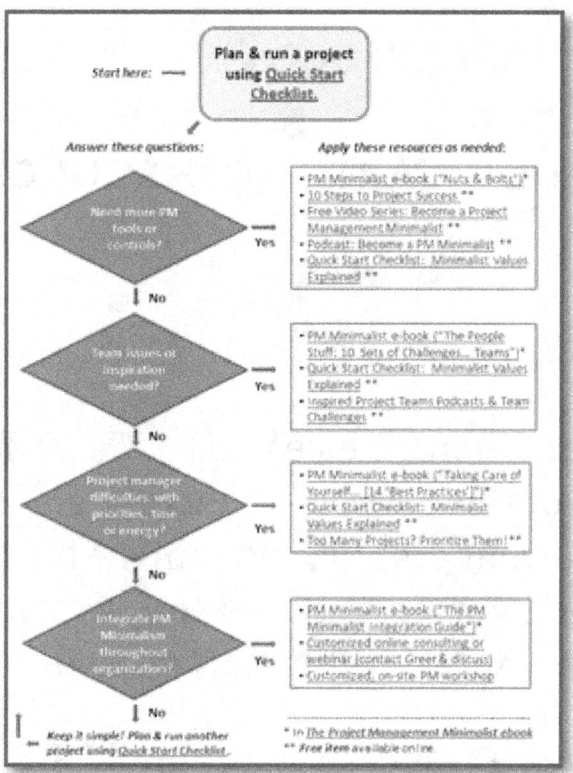

PDF Flowchart: **Applying PM Minimalism for Leaner PM** (It's loaded with links to other materials!)

(Flowchart URL: http://michaelgreer.biz/PM_Minimalist/Second-Edition-Support-Files/Flowchart-Applying-PM-Minimalism-for-Leaner-PM.pdf

"CUT THE FAT" AUDIT PART 1: THE SOURCES OF PM BLOAT

In this two-part series, I'll introduce you to **The PM Minimalist "Cut the Fat" Audit**. The goal of this audit is to uncover and eliminate the useless PM stuff that you and your organization might be doing — the stuff that swells up your projects for no good reason, wasting peoples' time and weighing down those who are trying to create your project deliverables.

Part 1: The Sources of Project Management Bloat

PM bloating manifests primarily in two forms:

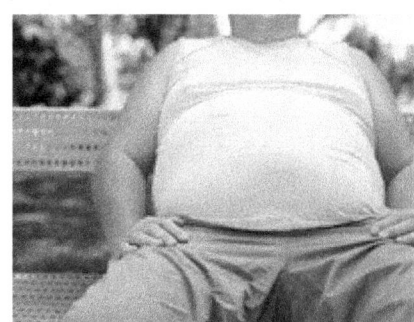

- Too many artifacts (i.e., schedules, worksheets, reports)
- Too much supervisory hovering

Too Many Artifacts

For most people, their first contact with Project Management (PM) comes as they squint their eyes and furrow their brows to decode that venerable, time-honored PM artifact, the Gantt chart. There it is! The entire project displayed all neat and tidy in a single graphic. Once they decode it, their heart reaches out in gratitude to this lovely little chart. They are relieved that it has finally summarized the chaos everyone's been describing as "our project" in a tight, easily apprehended little nutshell. This scary project may be doable after all! The Gantt gives hope, as well as the illusion of control.

Encouraged by the Gantt's near-magical powers, the PM novice quickly reaches out to other artifacts such as the Project Charter, WBS (Work Breakdown Structure), Scope Statement, tables showing staff responsibilities, schedules, cost estimates, and so on. These all share one commendable feature: They bring order to chaos and, in turn, stimulate confidence. Better yet, they can have a genuinely positive impact on the project by keeping the team focused and allowing the tracking of actual progress against the plan.

A downside of these artifacts, however, is that each one of them consumes a little time — time to create it, time to share and review it, time to react with feedback, time to finalize and time to revisit and maintain it. Worse, these artifacts can quietly grow roots and establish themselves as unquestioned members of the PM administrative process. As new projects unfold, the project managers each create, then deploy, their favorite artifacts. Sometimes they add their own to the organization's collection. Out of respect for the organization and its PM history, however, they seldom eliminate any. So **these things just accumulate like so many barnacles on an old boat hull**, with no one noticing the drag they create... or at least no one willing to complain openly. In fact, anyone complaining runs the risk of being regarded as either too lazy or too technically incompetent to create them. **The result: PM artifacts continue to pile up and weigh down project managers, project teams and, ultimately, the entire organization.**

Too Much Supervisory Hovering

One of the first things you notice about a small start-up organization's PM is the leanness of its project teams and processes. Lacking organizational depth, the start-up's projects run on the enthusiasm and vigilance of the people who are creating the deliverables. They don't have the luxury of a lot of roles; there are few, if any, supervisory levels. And there are few, if any, PM consultants, formally-titled Project Managers, or officially certified PM professionals. Running on the adrenalin that comes from pioneering and innovating, they simply synchronize themselves and get the work done.

Over time, if they are successful, the typical start-up grows larger as an organization and acquires more projects. Formal project roles emerge, with inspection processes, formal review cycles for evolving deliverables, formal life cycles, and prescribed management interventions and sign-offs. At first these roles and processes make sense as a means of adapting to the stress of the heavier work load and as a way of maintaining higher quality and greater consistency. **Unfortunately, over time and as the organizational PM culture evolves, these PM supervisory processes develop a life of their own.** Like the artifacts discussed above, the formalized roles and processes are welcomed at first because they keep things running more efficiently. But, also like the artifacts above, they can begin to accumulate as unquestioned elements of "the way we do things around here." Few managers are willing to challenge the organization to look back on the times when things were less formalized and more intuitive... less manager-heavy and more team-driven.

Eventually **an organization can reach the point where the people doing the work of creating deliverables are nearly outnumbered by the managers inspecting and intervening.** And as PM process is piled upon PM process, the time spent in creating deliverables can be overshadowed by the time spent in meetings, reviews, feedback sessions, and revision cycles. And unlike the excess artifacts discussed above, the excess processes and the excess managers typically are backed by considerably more political energy to maintain them. After all, **in the more mature organization, it's the PM consultants, formally-titled Project Managers, or officially certified PM professionals who have a deeply vested interest in these processes and managerial levels. So anyone trying to trim or eliminate them will likely find they have a fight on their hands.**

The result: PM processes and layers of PM management build up, dig in, grow roots, and develop ways of defending and perpetuating themselves.

What to Do: Look in the Mirror, Step on the Scales and Admit You've Got a Problem!

PM bloating and process-obesity can be treated! But the first step in treating it is to acknowledge it... to admit it exists. And that means having the courage to be a bit introspective — to take the time to document and analyze what's really going on in your projects.

In Part 2 of this series (... *A Project Management Weight Loss Strategy*), **I'll show you how you can conduct your own audit to distinguish fat from lean, reduce your bloated PM processes, and generally figure out how to cut the fat** and manage your projects Minimalist style.

"CUT THE FAT" AUDIT PART 2: A PM WEIGHT LOSS STRATEGY

In Part 1 of this series, *The Sources of Project Bloat*, I described how PM artifacts and processes typically accumulate over time and weigh down all of an organization's projects. In this article, I'll show you **how you can determine whether your organization's PM has become obese** and devise a customized **strategy to lose some PM weight.**

Part 2: A Project Management Weight Loss Strategy

So how can you figure out if your organization is PM process-heavy and weighed down by too many PM artifacts? The PM Minimalist "Cut the Fat" Audit can help. It consists of **three major activities:**

1. Inventory your active PM artifacts and processes.
2. Conduct the "Is This Really Valuable?" Analysis and the "Fix It or Ditch It?" Survey.
3. Develop your "Fix It or Ditch It" Recommendations.

Inventory Your Active PM Artifacts and Processes

Before you can decide which of your PM artifacts and processes are really useful and which contribute to PM bloat, you have **to figure out what's actually going on with your projects.** You need to develop an inventory. Here's how:

Step 1: Locate all of your organization's documents or policy statements that spell out the following:

- PM "best practices"

- Recommended Project Life Cycles

- Minimum requirements re: internal PM reviews and approvals

- Minimum requirements re: external (regulatory, legal, etc.) PM reviews and approvals

- PM minimum requirements related to staffing, equipment, support, etc.

Step 2: Locate as many actual project schedules as you can. Analyze these and determine common milestones, deliverables, PM practices, and so on. Specifically, look at:

- Project Phases

- Project "approval gates" (review & approval cycles)

- Generic deliverables (Project Charter, Project staffing plan, etc.)

- Any other common events that are assumed to be essential to every project

Step 3: Locate any actual PM artifacts related to project staffing. Analyze these and determine common assumptions made by all projects re:

- Staffing depth (numbers of people assigned to tasks, etc.)

- Internal quality assurance & review assignments

- External stakeholder or manager review assignments

- Any other assumptions about the roles and numbers of people assigned to projects

Step 4: Locate all key paperwork (approval forms, internal or external contracts, etc.) that typically tracks or validates your projects

- Forms used by senior management

- Forms used by financial, legal, HR, or other departments

- Forms used to coordinate with or legally bind customers

- Any other key paperwork that is required of projects

Step 5: Create a "Summary List of Project Management Processes and Artifacts" that enumerates everything you located in Steps 1 – 4. Subdivide this list into sections that cluster similar items together. For example your subsections might include:

- Required (Minimum) Project Phases

- Generic Project Deliverables (administrative requirements of all projects, no matter what they are creating)

- Required, or Minimum, Project Roles (i.e., essential team players for every project)

- Required Project Artifacts (Project Charter, Formal Proposal, Schedule, Budget, etc.)

- Required PM Practices (i.e., Practices employed on every project, no matter what the deliverables or schedule)

- Odd-but-common PM practices (i.e., Practices employed on some projects but we're not sure why)

After you've assembled this comprehensive list of PM artifacts and processes, you're ready to figure out which are worth keeping, which are in need of repair, and which should simply be dropped.

Conduct the "Is This Really Valuable?" Analysis and the "Fix It or Ditch It?" Survey

1. You've documented all your PM artifacts and processes. Now it's time to analyze them and figure out:

- Which of these artifacts and processes are valuable in their current form.

- Which need to be fixed or repaired. (i.e., Which might be more useful if they were revised in some way).

- Which should be ditched... eliminated entirely... because they are more trouble than they're worth.

Here's how you can answer these questions:

Step 1: Identify the people who work with all this PM stuff on a regular basis (project managers, subject matter experts, senior managers, client reviewers, project team members, administrative aids, etc.).

Step 2: Ask them all (or a broadly representative sample, if your organization is really large) to help you evaluate your PM artifacts and processes. Then ask them to complete an **"Is This Really Valuable?"** questionnaire with items like this:

PM Artifact/Process		*Check One:*	
Project Charter	☐ Valuable	☐ No opinion	☐ Not valuable
Weekly Status Report	☐ Valuable	☐ No opinion	☐ Not valuable
Daily QA Inspections	☐ Valuable	☐ No opinion	☐ Not valuable
Weekly Status Meetings	☐ Valuable	☐ No opinion	☐ Not valuable
Project Charter	☐ Valuable	☐ No opinion	☐ Not valuable
Etc., etc...	☐ Valuable	☐ No opinion	☐ Not valuable

Sample Items from the "Is This Really Valuable?" Analysis

(Be sure to include all the items you identified in your "Summary List of Project Management Processes and Artifacts," discussed earlier.)

Step 3: Obtain feedback from everyone and summarize their responses to the questionnaires. (You'll be using this summary info in the next step.)

Step 4: Create and circulate a **"Fix It or Ditch It" Questionnaire** that includes items like this:

PM Artifact/Process	_Check One:_		
Project Charter • Valuable: 75% • No opinion: 15% • Not valuable: 10%	☐ Ditch it	☐ Fix it	_(If fix it...)_ List your suggested improvements:
Weekly Status Report • Valuable: 80% • No opinion: 15% • Not valuable: 5%	☐ Ditch it	☐ Fix it	_(If fix it...)_ List your suggested improvements:
Daily QA Inspections • Valuable: 35% • No opinion: 10% • Not valuable: 55%	☐ Ditch it	☐ Fix it	_(If fix it...)_ List your suggested improvements:

Sample Items on a "Fix It or Ditch It" Questionnaire

Note that **the left column** presents the **results** of your "Is This Really Valuable?" analysis. By including this information, those responding to the survey can see how others in your organization feel about each artifact or process they are evaluating. With this background information as context for their decision, they are asked to decide whether your organization should "Ditch it" (i.e., eliminate the artifact or process entirely) or "Fix it" (i.e., improve the artifact or process). If respondents choose "Fix it," they are also asked to provide their specific suggestions for how the item might be fixed.

Develop your "Fix It or Ditch It" Recommendations

At this point you've developed quite a collection of input from members of your organization about your PM artifacts and processes. Now it's time to do something with these recommendations. Specifically, you might:

- **Rank order the the PM artifacts and processes that should be "ditched" and summarize them** in a comprehensive list. Present this list to senior management, along with your recommendations for abandoning them. Then **formally decide, as a management team, which ought to be abandoned.** (Note: If senior management is reluctant to abandon some items, suggest that you try abandoning them on a few test projects and see if these items are missed. If not, then you can go ahead and discontinue their use throughout the organization.)

- **Summarize all the "fix it" items,** along with respondents suggestions for fixing them. **Ask for volunteers to work together to create the repairs to PM artifacts or to develop guidelines for streamlining and improving PM processes.** (Ask the people who provided you with the most thoughtful suggestions for improvement to "volunteer" for this repair work.)

- **Get everyone together** who helped with the analysis and **tell them how things have changed as a result of their input.** If it makes sense, develop a few *brief* guidelines that reflect your new, leaner approach. (But be careful not to generate more PM bloat!)

Conclusion

Anyone who has ever lost weight and kept it off knows that it takes an entire lifestyle change. It's not simply a one-time event. Similarly, **The PM Minimalist approach to reducing your organization's PM fat is not a one-time event.** Like the dieter who is continually tempted by high-fat desserts and buffets, your organization will be continually encouraged by PM consultants and "experts" to add layers of complexity to your PM.

Dieters learn to say "No" to temptation, all the while monitoring their weight and maintaining a healthy diet and exercise program. Similarly, **your PM leaders need to learn to say "No" to PM "experts" and periodically conduct their own "Cut the Fat" audits as part of your organization's quest for PM Minimalism.**

The good new is that **by repeatedly asking everyone "Is this really valuable?" you will be encouraging a healthy skepticism among your PM practitioners** that can, in effect, establish **a PM Minimalist "cut-the-PM-fat" support group.** This way, when anyone tries to pile on a new PM artifact or process, there is likely to be someone ready to push back and ask, "Is this really, truly valuable and worth our time and effort?"

As more people stand up and defend PM Minimalism, you'll eventually all come to enjoy the benefits of a leaner, healthier PM culture.

THE PROJECT MANAGEMENT CHANGE AGENT: HOW TO LEAD YOUR PM REVOLUTION

(Note: This is an overview of a free video & PDF which can help you create your own unique PM revolution.)

Overview

Is your organization ready for a project management (PM) revolution?

Specifically:

- Are your projects always running late, over budget, and plagued by "do overs?"

- Do people hate working on your project teams and try to avoid being assigned to projects?

- Are you continually reworking and reworking deliverables because you just can't seem to get it right in the first place?

- And if it is time for a PM revolution, then where should you begin?

This video and accompanying PDF is for everyone who wants to be the change agent who brings about a PM revolution in their organization. Whether you are a middle manager, HR professional, supervisor, or simply a task specialist who wants to conduct some "below the radar" guerrilla PM warfare, you can benefit from this video & the summary PDF.

Topics

Specifically, the **54-minute video and 25-page PDF address these topics:**

- 5 Signs You're Ready for a Project Management Revolution
- 5 levels of PM Sophistication for an Organization
- 5 Levels of PM Sophistication for Project Managers
- 5 Levels of Sophistication Re: PM Training & Performance Support
- The Arguments Against PM Change
- The PM Revolution: Exploding Bombs and Growing Bougainvilleas

  ◦ Some Powerful "PM Change" Bombs

  ◦ 8 Change-Inducing PM Tools

  ◦ 10 Stealthy, "Vining" PM Practices

- What Absolutely Won't Work
- Bomb or Bougainvillea: Criteria for Success
- The Role of PM Training and Certification (& Why Certification May Not Matter)
- Start Your PM Revolution: 10 Steps
- Resources That Can Help

Links to free video and PDF:

- **54-minute Video:** http://vimeo.com/channels/michaelgreer/ 60418162
- **25-Page PDF**: http://michaelgreer.biz/M-Greers-The-Project-Management-Change-Agent-Selected-Visuals-2-25-2013.pdf

THE PM MINIMALIST INTEGRATION GUIDE: ADOPTING PROJECT MANAGEMENT MINIMALISM IN YOUR ORGANIZATION

In the last chapter you were encouraged to try "going Minimalist" with one or more of your own projects. If you're ready to try to get Project Management Minimalism adopted throughout your organization, this tool can help.

The PM Minimalist Integration Guide provides an easy-to-follow, step-by-step process that you can use to gradually integrate Project Management Minimalist practices into your organization. Specifically, it will guide you through **three Stages of PM Minimalist Integration:**

- Integration **Stage 1: Proof of Concept**

- Integration **Stage 2: Limited Practice**

- Integration **Stage 3: Extended Practice**

Download the 7-page PM Minimalist Integration Guide.* *(URL: http://michaelgreer.biz/PM-Minimalist-Integration-Guide-Ver-1.pdf)*

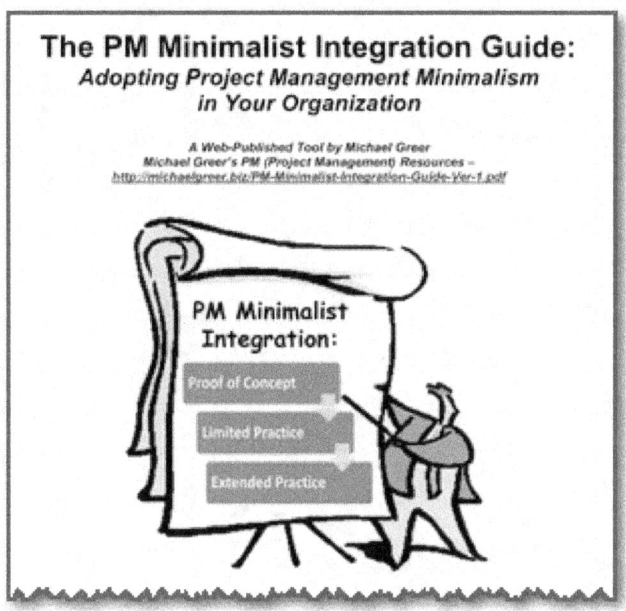

Download the 7-page PDF: ***The PM Minimalist Integration Guide*** *

---

* *The PM Minimalist Integration Guide is an excerpt from the book,* ***The Project Management Minimalist: Just Enough PM to Rock Your Projects!***

OF PM SKILLS AND HOW THEY ARE ACQUIRED

This Part examines, in some detail, the important skills needed to manage projects, how project managers acquire these skills and how their organizations can help them to do so more effectively.

Caveat re: This Part

The Good News: I started out my professional life as an instructional designer and HPT (Human Performance Technology) guy. That means I care deeply about how people acquire practical, job-related skills, as opposed to spending a lot of time learning esoteric "content" that they may or may not be able to use on the job. *(i.e., for me, job performance & skills are key!)*

The Bad News: Some of the articles collected in this section were written for training and HR people who, like any group of professionals, have their own jargon. So the ***discussion points and recommendations may occasionally drift into the training & HR "weeds."***

THE ACCIDENTAL PROJECT MANAGER

Introduction

This article is intended for a particular kind of project management (PM) newcomer –someone I call the accidental project manager. It is intended to provide these folks with encouragement and hope!

Are you an accidental project manager?

Here are **some tell-tale signs:**

- Primarily because of your competence in your technical specialty or your profession, **you suddenly find yourself responsible for managing a project** for your organization. (Maybe you didn't duck fast enough when they were choosing a team leader... or maybe you have informally demonstrated leadership without having the formal job title of leader or manager and they decided it was time to "put you in charge.")

- **You know your profession** and you have a pretty good idea of the kinds of results (i.e., the finished product or customer impact) you want your project to achieve.

- While you're not really sure if you want to manage the project, **you have a strong sense of professional pride and you know you would like your project to achieve quality results** (as defined by your profession), on-time, and within budget.

- **You will probably be serving as project manager or team leader**

at the same time you are making your own contribution to the project as a specialist in your field (in other words, you may be managing the project on a part-time basis).

- You have had **little or no formal training in PM.**

- You are **somewhat suspicious that maybe "all that formal project management stuff" is maybe overkill** and might just be a bunch of joyless "administrivia" that will stifle the creativity of your team

- Still, **you have a feeling some PM discipline will probably be useful** to your project, but you're not quite sure how much or what form it should take.

- You are **certain you have no need to learn** all the **sophisticated management techniques** that a project manager would need to manage a billion-dollar construction project or to land a space craft on Mars.

- You are **looking for practical, no-nonsense tools and techniques** that will help you do "just enough" PM to keep things running smoothly — and no more!

- For now, at least, you are certain that **you aren't interested in pursuing project manager certification from asapm, PMI, PRINCE2, or any other certifying body.** Instead, you see the evolution of your career in terms of acquiring broader and deeper knowledge of your chosen specialty.

OK. You're an accidental project manager. Is there hope for you?

If most of the above statements seem to apply to you, then you are most likely an accidental project manager. And I'd like to assure you that it's okay for your eyes to glaze over and your jaws to stifle a silent yawn when you are in the presence of people who are discussing the finer points of one or another PM certification test. After all, what revs up your engine is the latest and greatest technical innovation in your specialty! So it's perfectly reasonable to wish that the PM gurus would "get to the point, already!"

To understand where the accidental project manager fits within the field of PM, it is useful to step outside the PM realm and **consider, by way of analogy, the field of medicine.** In the medical field, as in PM, there are all sorts of skill-levels required of its various practitioners. For example, medical researchers seek cures and develop clinical protocols (i.e., medical "best practices") which are implemented by highly-trained surgeons, specialists, and family doctors. Emergency medical technicians make critical interventions applying these clinical protocols in order to keep people alive long enough to turn them over to the care of these more highly-trained specialists. At the same time, in small towns and rural communities all over the world, volunteer fire fighters and other local first responders apply emergency first aid to accident victims in the form of CPR and other easily-trainable medical procedures. And finally, parents, coaches, and scout leaders apply similar first aid to the minor wounds and medical emergencies suffered by their kids.

The point is, you don't need to be trained in the subtleties of cell physiology or cardio-pulmonary surgery to perform CPR and save a life. You just need to have the right tool or procedure and the confidence to apply it. And the same is true for you, the accidental project manager. You need not be able to recite all possible PM definitions and terms to achieve great results in your role as project leader or part-time project manager. Let your joy and professional satisfaction come from applying **just enough PM** to help your team achieve high-quality results from projects in your specialty.

Relax! You already know enough to make a difference!

In my PM Basics workshops I spend a lot of time working with accidental project managers. The vast majority of these folks are highly effective in their specialties — otherwise, their senior management wouldn't be investing in developing their PM skills. Unfortunately, these PM novices often find themselves intimidated by the concepts, structures, and field-specific terminology associated with the PM profession. If you are feeling this way, I urge you to relax and remember the many roles played in the medical profession. More to the point, remember the volunteer fire fighter or scout leader. In times of emergency, these people make invaluable contributions at the entry levels of the medical field — indeed, they save lives! Yet they certainly don't expect themselves to know everything the doctors know. Instead, they focus their efforts on learning exactly the right basic medical procedures to get immediate, high-quality results. Are they ashamed because they don't have the depth of knowledge as the medical researcher or surgeon? Certainly not! In their "real professions" they may be lawyers, accountants, computer techs, or whatever... and they could undoubtedly teach medical experts a thing or two about these specialties.

So welcome, accidental project manager, to the sometimes complex, sometimes helpful, sometimes overblown world of formal PM. **As you wander through the PM world, give yourself permission to be lost, even confused. And give yourself permission to pick and choose the kinds of things that will help you manage your projects more effectively. Above all, use your common sense and your in-depth knowledge of your primary specialty, to help you reject the PM stuff that you know won't help your projects.** After all, most of PM's best practices are rooted in common sense; they are the simple practices of experienced people, wrapped up in sometimes high-sounding terms. And the good news is that because PM is rooted in common sense, it is fairly easy to learn.

Remember the Scarecrow?

Finally, **remember the Scarecrow from the Wizard of Oz?** More than anything else, he wanted to have a brain... he wanted to be brilliant. But by simply testing himself in the quest to save Dorothy, he discovered he already had all the wisdom he needed. He only had to reach inside himself and apply it. **He didn't really need the Wizard to validate this wisdom. Nor do you need the great and powerful PM professionals to validate your inherent wisdom.** You merely need to find some PM tools and procedures that seem useful, decipher them, filter them through your professional experiences, and put them to work for your project team. Informed by your inherent wisdom, you will most likely achieve excellent results.

PROJECT MANAGEMENT IS A BROAD HUMAN PRACTICE, NOT MERELY A PROFESSION.

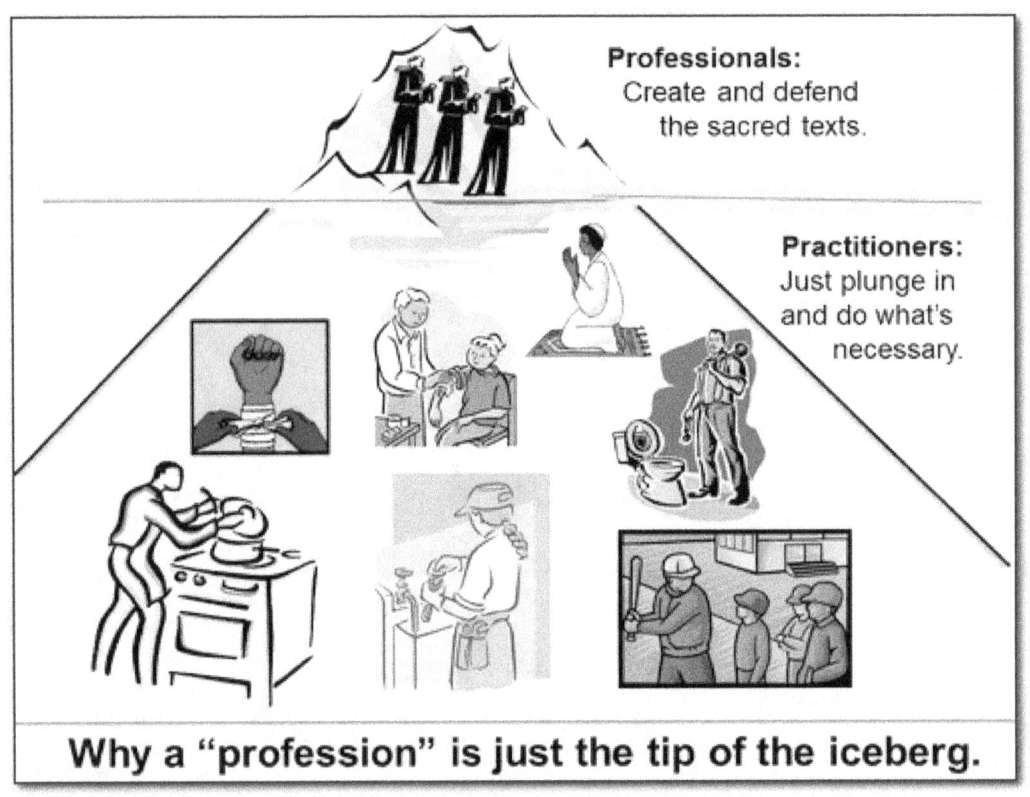

Professionals: Create and defend the sacred texts.

Practitioners: Just plunge in and do what's necessary.

Why a "profession" is just the tip of the iceberg.

In a recent post at The PM Hut titled *Defending the Project Management Profession** Bruce McGraw wrote: "… having recently seen ads for fast, cheap and simple project management training and tools, I felt the need to state firmly my position on this matter… [that] project management is a profession and project managers are professionals." OK. Fair enough. Then Bruce goes on to provide ample evidence that PM is indeed a profession.

But I feel compelled to add: **"Yes… AND… project management is**

much more than a mere profession: It's a broad practice undertaken by many, many of our fellow humans. And, as a broadly undertaken practice, there is a compelling need for 'fast, cheap, and simple PM training and tools.'" That's because the majority of PM practitioners are people who are just jumping in and getting the job done, without giving a second thought to the PM profession, PM professionals or their vocabulary and "shoulds." And any tools or training that these people find helpful (including fast, cheap, or simple ones) are by definition valuable.

A Bit on the Evolution of Professions & Professionals

We humans are problem-solvers. We do all sorts of things to improve our circumstances and remove obstacles to our success. Some of these things we do are so fascinating to us that we begin to share our problem-solving techniques with each other, comparing notes, developing methodologies, and archiving our strategies. Eventually, in some domains, there are a few individuals who become so captivated by working with a particular kind of problem that they decide to make it a full-time pursuit. And inevitably, though the problem they are solving has its roots in common, shared human experiences, these **"full-timers" begin to regard themselves as a class apart from the rest of us. They begin to regard themselves as professionals. And they label the thing they do as a "profession."**

The trouble with professionals, however, is that it's easy for them to lose touch with two simple facts:

1. **The rest of humanity continues to solve problems in the professional's domain on a daily basis.** (Every day they "practice" achieving practical, necessary results so they can get on with their lives.)
2. **The rest of humanity uses (and demands) the simplest, most common-sense techniques that get the job done.** They simply

do what works. And though non-professionals may not have developed sophisticated (or arcane?) terminology to describe their techniques, the techniques nonetheless work. They get results.

In short, **most domains of human activity begin as broad, human practices... a set of actions that work to get results. Eventually, in some domains, a sort of "high priest" class evolves who study the domain deeply, analyze it beyond what ordinary folks would choose to do, and anoint themselves as "professionals"** who are uniquely qualified to practice in this domain. Meanwhile, ordinary people go on about their lives, getting things done and picking and choosing the professionally-recommended "best practices" that make sense to them.

Let's Get Real: Some Typical Human Practices & Their "Professional" Corollaries

Here are some examples to illustrate the dynamic described above. **All of the activities listed below are common human practices; all of them are things that we all do to somehow enrich our lives or solve problems. Yet all generate their own "professional" class of practitioners.**

- **Cooking:** Everybody prepares food for themselves. At the same time, professionally-certified chefs are schooled in food chemistry, heating/cooking strategies, the art of combining flavors, etc.

- **Treatment of Injury or Disease:** Everybody treats their own injuries or diseases. (They stop the bleeding. They apply medications, etc.). And most of us will inevitably provide first-aid treatment for someone else. At the same time, a fascinated few delve deeply into medical research and learn to treat medical problems as medical professionals.

- **Plumbing:** Everybody at one time or another hooks up a garden hose or struggles to keep their toilet working. Some people perform minor plumbing repairs around the house. And some do-it-yourselfers go so far as to build or modify their own plumbing systems. At the same time, highly-trained plumbers study plumbing and the design of water/drainage techniques so that they can build and repair complex plumbing systems. They become professional plumbers.

- **Writing:** Everybody writes letters and reports. Some folks study writing techniques and learn to use sophisticated writing tools and processes. Some folks become professional writers.

- **Teaching:** Every parent teaches basic concepts to their children. And every parent coaches on an ad-hoc basis. Yet some people choose to spend all day, every day, teaching or coaching. These folks become professional educators, trainers, or coaches.

- **Leadership:** Every parent has, at one time or another, acted as a leader for her children. Parents articulate a goal or vision, motivate, cajole, inspect progress, and lead the way to achieving the goal. At the same time, students of management and would-be executives can spend years studying leadership as a part of their senior management training so they can lead in a "professional" way.

- **Prayer:** Everybody who wants to do so can (and does) talk to their God. Despite the universality of this practice, a class of individuals who have spent their lives studying theology and spirituality (priests, rabbis, ayatollahs, ministers, monks, and the like) stand ready to help us figure out new ways to relate to our various dieties.

- **Project Management:** **Kids** who are completing complex class assignments are informally managing projects. **Leaders in civic organizations** who complete local fund raising efforts must informally manage these as projects. **Small business owners** routinely practice project management. Though they would rather practice their industry specialty than study PM, they realize that they must perform "just enough" PM to get things done and remain competitive. Indeed, managers in all sorts of large organizations in all sorts of industries manage project after project every day in order to complete their assignments. All of these people **do what they have to do to get the job done.** Still, at the same time, many different PM professional associations and their members stand ready to help "professionalize" the practice of project management and provide people who can help deal with complex PM problems.

So (once again... for emphasis!)... **Project management is much more than a mere profession: It's a broad practice undertaken by many, many of our fellow humans. And, as a broadly undertaken practice, there is a compelling need for "fast, cheap, and simple PM training and tools"** precisely because the majority of PM practitioners are people who are just jumping in and getting the job done, without giving a second thought to the PM profession, PM professionals or their vocabulary and "shoulds." **So any tool or training that these people find helpful (including fast, cheap, or simple ones) are by definition valuable.**

———————

*	Link	details: http://www.pmhut.com/defending-the-project-management-profession

HOW TO GET YOUR FIRST JOB IN PROJECT MANAGEMENT (PM)

I was recently corresponding with Geoff Crane, the creative force behind The Papercut Project Manager website, about how people can get started in Project Management (PM). After some thought-provoking back and forth with him on the topic, I was inspired to create the following article. (Thanks, Geoff!)

In more than three decades of working with PM newbies in my classes, I've heard a lot of great stories about how people became project managers. Based on what I've heard, I have **two broad suggestions** for anyone who would like to get that first job as a project manager:

1. **Become a valuable and trusted contributor on project teams.**

2. **"Act as if" you are in charge** of (or at least responsible for) one or more projects.

Here's a closer look each of these.

Become a Valuable and Trusted Project Contributor

Something every would-be project manager ought to consider: PM is an activity that is often regarded as "overhead." That means that the time project managers spend on their PM chores is budgeted under "administrative costs" or a similar heading. In contrast, the primary work of creating project deliverables is typically done by specialists in a given field. The scriptwriters, computer programmers, researchers, systems analysts, plumbers and electricians, etc. – all these folks make unique contributions that are based on their mastering a chosen specialty. Over time, if they do good work, they come to be regarded as valuable and trusted project contributors. They are the "go to" people who get things done, know how to deal with obstacles and can creatively invent short-cuts that can be implemented without sacrificing quality.

Now **if you are going to manage a project in a given field, you need to have developed a substantial working knowledge of that field for two primary reasons:**

1. Your **detailed plans, inspections, reviews and client/ stakeholder outreach** efforts need to make sense within the context of that field and its professional "best practices" **and,**
2. You need to have the respect of those key project contributors **so that when you ask them to do something they trust that you know what you're talking about and will comply. And the best way to get their respect is if you, yourself, have spent some time working shoulder-to-shoulder with them, getting good results.**

So whether you're trying to create an accurate task list and matching project schedule, trying to sell the project to stakeholders whose support you need or trying to nudge project team members to take a specific course of action, it really helps to have spent some time yourself as a project team member, making valuable contributions and earning the trust of your peers, SMEs and other stakeholders. (And it also helps if you love this field, can empathize with the passions of its practitioners and truly enjoy working with them!)

"Act as If" You Are Responsible

In his book *The Power of Intention*, Wayne Dyer suggests that we: "Act as if everything you desire is already here... treat yourself as if you already are what you'd like to become." And in his book, *Get Out of Your Own Way*, Robert K. Cooper writes: "Brain scans show that simply imagining a complex and compelling goal will actually fire the same neurons that will be required to actually achieve the goal... In order to sense a new idea or shape a better future, we must first create it in the brain as a possibility..."

Translating these high-sounding suggestions to our topic of getting a foothold in PM (and getting a bit more specific) here is **a list of things I've observed that "ordinary" project team members were doing just before they broke into their official role of project manager:**

- **Anticipating problems** that the team might face, then helping to prevent them

- **Going beyond simply enduring or complaining** about obstacles or roadblocks **to taking the actions** that were necessary **to help remove them**

- Filling in the gaps by **doing the dirty, thankless jobs** when no one else was available in order to keep the project moving

- Stepping up and acting on behalf of — or, more specifically, **acting as if they "owned"**:

  - The **schedule**

  - The budget

  - The **resource work load** that may have needed balancing

  - The **quality** of the finished product

- **Advocating on behalf of team members** who wouldn't (or couldn't) speak up for themselves

- **Serving as a bridge between stakeholders and the professionals on the project team** by helping translate technical jargon, explain field-specific best practices or generally selling the project and its value

- **Leading**, in critical moments **when there was no one else around to serve as leader**

In short, when a member of the project team starts doing the kinds of things listed above, the senior managers and stakeholders who are orbiting the project begin to listen more carefully when this person speaks. And eventually this person acquires the personal gravitas to be asked to serve, officially, as a project manager.

Like a Glacier

If you practice the two broad collections of behaviors discussed above, it is almost inevitable that you acquire the job title of project manager. And this job title will be deserved because you have authentically:

- Mastered a profession and **earned the respect of your peers** through a track record of competence

- **Become a de facto project manager by "acting as if"** you own and take responsibility for the projects on which you work

Do these things and slowly but surely, with the inevitability of a glacier moving inexorably down a mountain, you will become a project manager.

Related chapters/podcasts

- **Project Management is a Broad Human Practice, not Merely a Profession** *(Chapter 48 in this book)*

- **Podcast: Act As If** — http://www.inspiredprojectteams.com/?p=666

- **Podcast: Trust Your Judgment** — http://www.inspiredprojectteams.com/?p=691

- **Podcast: Just Do It!** — http://www.inspiredprojectteams.com/?p=724

HOW TO TEACH YOURSELF ABOUT PROJECT MANAGEMENT WITHOUT SPENDING ANY MONEY ON TRAINING OR CONSULTANTS

*[**Note:** If you're in a hurry to get started learning about PM, check out my online fast-track article "How to Teach Yourself About Project Management... in Under 3 Hours (and for less than $10)!!" On the other hand, the "teach yourself" process outlined below is more of a "deep dive" and will take a little longer.]*

I am often contacted by people who are new to project management (PM) and who would like the names of textbooks or other references that can help them learn about PM. These people aren't ready to commit to a formal PM class, but would like to do some intelligent investigation of the PM field on their own. Because I'm a trainer at heart and I know that it's not enough to simply read about something to learn about it, I recommend the following mixture of reading and self-guided activities. I hope you find these to be helpful.

1. Obtain a couple of good, basic PM references that you can revisit frequently.

You don't need to read these documents entirely, simply have them at hand to examine as questions arise. I recommend the following free documents:

- The Project Management Institute's ***A Guide to the Project Management Body of Knowledge (PMBOK)*** – This document, put together by PMI's Standards Committee, identifies and provides basic descriptions of nearly every proven and generally accepted PM practice. You will probably revisit it regularly to provide you with either PM fundamentals or broader PM context as you consider a particular PM author's recommendations. I keep mine on my desk beside my dictionary and use it all the time. You can download this free from this web site at http://www.cs.bilkent.edu.tr/~cagatay/cs413/PMBOK.pdf

  - ***(NOTE:*** If you're thinking about pursuing PMI's PMP (project management professional) certification, check out my video tour of some great free online training that can help you see what you're getting into. See Stuck Pursuing PMP Certification? Take Firebrand Training for Free! [A Video Tour])

- **American Society for the Advancement of Project Management's (asapm) Competency Model** provides "The Competency Framework: A structured list of the minimum competencies that Project Managers and key stakeholders must demonstrate—with the target competency levels for each." While PMI's PMBOK (above) defines essential PM Knowledge areas, asapm's Competency Model focuses on what those involved in PM must be able to do to get the job done. It identifies "... roles of Project Manager 1 (Team Leaders or managers of small projects), Project Manager 2 (medium or large, but less-complex projects) and Project Manager 3 (Managers of large, complex Projects and Programs)" as well as the roles of other stakeholders, including sponsor, resource manager, Project Office staff, and project team members.

- ***The Project Management Forum's PM Glossary*** by Max Wideman – This amazing, frequently-updated on-line reference tool provides definitions of nearly any PM term or concept you are likely to encounter, along with a specific citation of the source from which the definition is drawn. Frequently, there are several different definitions of the same term, depending on the reference cited. You should bookmark this powerful source and visit it whenever you are learning a new PM term or concept.

2. Do some broad study to get an overview of PM.

I recommend the following free or low cost resources:

- This **free PDF** document: 10 Steps to Project Success (from The Project Management Minimalist)

- These **free videos** (use the above "10 Steps…" PDF document as a reference): Free Video Series: Become a Project Management Minimalist (8 videos, less than 1 hour total)

- This **free, 37-minute podcast**: Become a Project Management Minimalist (includes Team Challenges)

- *Part I: The Project Management Framework* in PMI's A Guide to PMBOK. The three chapters contained in this section of the Guide will provide a broad overview of the larger management context in which PM takes place and will provide an overview of PM processes.

- Summary of Key Project Manager Actions & Results. This free handout, available from my website, will help you see in specific performance terms what results project managers should be achieving and the specific actions which they should take to achieve those results.

- 14 Key Principles for PM Success. This free handout, also available from my website, will help you get a sense of some of the more important underlying principles or values which successful project managers share.

… and the following low-cost resources:

- ***The Project Management Minimalist: Just Enough PM to Rock Your Projects!***

- ANY of the free PM books, podcasts and references listed at my **Project Management FREEBIES website.**

3. Informally evaluate your own or your organization's current PM practices.

After you've completed steps 1 & 2 above, you might want to see how well some of these PM fundamentals are being practiced in your organization. Below are a couple of free tools that you can use to organize your thoughts and guide your analysis. Depending on your local management context, you could simply use these tools yourself and reflect on your findings or you could seek broader input from stakeholders, project team members, customers, or senior managers. Either way, applying one of these tools will help you figure out what PM concepts and practices you need to learn more about.

- *Project "Post Mortem" Review Questions* – This set of questions can help you reflect on what went wrong, what went right, and what needs improving in your PM efforts.

- *Critical Attributes of ID Project Success* – If you develop training or documentation, you can compare your PM practices to those identified in this list. The more of these practices your team employs, the greater your chance of project success.

4. Find some examples of well-organized project plans and figure out what you can learn (or borrow) from them.

Contact people in your organization or your industry who have created successful project plans and ask them to share these plans with you. Better yet, if their project plans are on disk, ask them to give you the files so you can use them as templates for planning your own projects.

Typically, project plans are in Word, Excel, or MS Project file formats, so you can easily open them with your own software and edit them. Look for examples of project charters, project schedules, work breakdown structures (WBS), lists of deliverables, lists of phases or activities, resource lists, and so on. As you examine each of them, ask yourself, "How could I adapt this approach to improve my next project plan? ... to improve my next PM tracking effort?"

- You can find lots of good free stuff in the Templates/Tools collection at my Project Management FREEBIES website.

5. Now go plan and manage your own project.

At this point, you're ready for some real-world practice. So gather up all the tools, guidelines, checklists, and so forth that you've acquired in the preceding steps and put them to work. For more specific, in-depth help along the way, including worksheets, guidelines, etc., you might want to revisit the texts I mentioned in Step 2, above. In particular, my book, *The Project Management Minimalist: Just Enough PM to Rock Your Projects!*, has most of the essential PM tools to help you create important project artifacts. Finally, the second edition of my book *The Project Manager's Partner* contains a total of 57 tools, worksheets, and so on to help you plan and manage projects.

And finally, if you've like to take a lean "Minimalist" approach to your first project, just follow the steps in this article in in this book: ***Be a Role Model of PM Minimalism: Manage Your Projects with a One-Page Checklist!***

BEYOND PM CERTIFICATION: ACHIEVING PM PERFORMANCE IMPROVEMENT

(Note: The primary audience of this chapter is the person who is responsible for establishing and maintaining an organization's training and development efforts – particularly as these relate to project management (PM). A secondary audience might be someone working with an organization's project management office [PMO] who wants to create a structured PM career path to be monitored and supported by the PMO.)

Introduction: A Stranger in a Strange Land

The last couple of days have been intellectually turbulent, but at the same time exhilarating. After more than 25 years teaching and writing about project management, I've come to realize exactly why I've sometimes had the disturbing feeling of being a stranger in a strange land. The catalyst of this powerful, and overdue, realization has been **Dr. Paul D. Giammalvo's** incredible paper ***Project Management Credentials Compared – A Preliminary Analysis.*** (This has been the basis of a PM-related group discussion at LinkedIn.)

In this paper, Dr. Giammalvo undertakes a preliminary comparison of many different project management (PM) credentials available from several professional organizations that are "generally recognized around the world." These include "... (in alphabetical order):

- American Society for the Advancement of Project Management (asapm)

- Association for the Advancement of Cost Engineering International (AACE)

- Australian Institute of Project Management (AIPM)

- International Council of Systems Engineers (INCOSE)

- OGC/APM's PRINCE2

- Project Management Institute (PMI)"

Dr. Giammalvo explains: "This list is NOT all inclusive, nor was it intended to be, but it was felt that it represents the more commonly recognized credentials in the field of project/program management." His purpose was "to see if it was feasible to produce a meaningful ratio scale against which to rank order and compare the relative standings of the various credentials."

Amazingly, after struggling with this highly-complex challenge, **Dr. Giammalvo finally was able to rank order the various PM certifications based on the amount of effort and formal degrees required to obtain them.**

So, for example, he is able to show that:

"... PRINCE2 credentials are significantly lower than all other credentials, while at the other extreme, AACE's top credentials, the C3PM and the CFCC scored very high."

And he is also able to defend such assertions as:

"... the top ranked credentials are NOT coming from PMI, which is without question the largest and most influential of the professional organizations purporting to represent practitioners of project management, but are dominated by the much less well known organizations..."

As I continued to review Dr. Giammalvo's findings, it hit me! I knew exactly why I've sometimes felt such a stranger in this strange land of PM. It is because **over the years I have been denying that little voice inside me that has been quietly repeating that this PM certification and credentialing stuff is maybe beside the point – that it's almost irrelevant. Or worse, that it sometimes appears to be designed primarily to meet the needs of those creating, bestowing, teaching, and consulting about the credentials** instead of meeting the needs of those who practice project and program management.

In short, I came to realize that PM certification and credentialing is not really meant to achieve true PM performance improvement. And, since PM performance improvement is what I really care about, I yawn, fidget in my seat, and sometimes even get mildly annoyed when my PM colleagues or clients begin to drone on and on about arcane subtleties and esoterica related to the various PM certification and credentialing processes.

So Why Focus on Performance Improvement?

My obsession with performance improvement comes from many years of professional practice as an instructional designer, curriculum analyst and performance improvement professional prior to my writing PM texts and consulting in PM. In a career now exceeding three decades, I've completed many training needs analyses, analyzed sets of job-related competencies, developed job models and career paths, erected curriculum architectures, and created training and tools to support the acquisition of new skills by both PM and non-PM workers.

I've worked with a lot of change agents in organizations who were struggling to achieve organization-specific performance improvement. **And this I know for sure: At their best, external credentials and certifications shed light and provide some valuable guidance on internal training and career development needs. At their worst,** they become troublesome collections of criteria that can be extremely difficult to "sync up" with internal, organization-specific performance improvement efforts and strategic initiatives.

If the professionals who are practicing PM and advocating for more professional approaches to PM are to have real, meaningful impact in improving the real-world performance of PM as it is practiced in organizations, they must come to view HR and training people as their prime customers. These members of what I call "the PM Profession" must provide HR and training people with:

- **A consistent, "shaken down," and synthesized collection of PM competencies** that will help internal HR/training people flesh out specific PM-related job descriptions, roles, and responsibilities.

- **Tools, tools, and more tools** in the form of worksheets, templates, guidelines, protocols, and procedures **that support PM "best practices"** in different industries.

- **An end to the proliferation and duplication of PM credentials and confusing certification** practices by synthesizing **a single set of generic, universally-acceptable PM competencies, tools, and certifications.**

By providing these three items, and making them freely available, the PM Profession will become partners with organizations everywhere in helping to create true PM performance improvement.

PM is for Everyone, Not Just Professionals

Some of what is troubling to me about current PM certification and credentialing is that it is exclusionary. Those who achieve these are part of one or another select club. Yet, whether the PM Profession likes it or not, PM itself is ubiquitous and it is practiced by nearly everyone at one time or another, formally or informally. Therefore, **what is needed from**

the PM Profession is not a set of artificial boundaries separating the various levels of PM performers, but rather professional tools and guidance to help those tasked with PM to do a better job.

There are **two fields which can serve as powerful analogies to help illustrate how PM might be made accessible to everyone,** not just a handful of selected and certified professionals:

- The practice of medicine

- The practice of physical fitness

In the field of medicine, as in PM, there are all sorts of skill-levels required of its various practitioners. For example, medical researchers seek cures and develop clinical protocols (i.e., medical "best practices") which are implemented by highly-trained surgeons, specialists, and family doctors. Emergency medical technicians make critical interventions by applying these clinical protocols in order to keep people alive long enough to turn them over to the care of these more highly-trained specialists. At the same time, in small towns and rural communities all over the world, volunteer fire fighters and other local first responders apply emergency first aid to accident victims in the form of CPR and other easily-trainable medical procedures. And finally, ordinary citizens in their roles as parents, coaches, and scout leaders apply similar first aid to the minor wounds and medical emergencies suffered by their kids.

A similar hierarchy of practice may be found in the physical fitness field. Medical researchers scrutinize what works and what doesn't work to achieve maximum levels of fitness. They then hand off this information to physical therapists and team physicians who work with patients and athletes to apply the best practices suggested by the research. Finally, some of these physicians and physical therapists write books or articles containing nice, tight summaries (recipes, protocols, checklists, etc.) that may be applied by anyone seeking greater levels of physical fitness.

The point is, you don't need to be trained in the subtleties of cell physiology or cardio-pulmonary surgery to practice first aid, perform CPR, and save a life. Nor do you need to be a sophisticated medical researcher to design and implement your own physical fitness program. You just need to have the right tools or procedures and the confidence to apply them.

And the same is true for anybody practicing project management – even the greenest of PM newbies. They need not be able to recite all possible PM definitions and terms or unravel arcane problems of earned value analysis to achieve great results in their roles as project leaders or part-time project managers. They simply need good tools and procedures, as well as some locally-relevant training and coaching on how these should be applied. In fact, in their primary roles as proud practitioners of a particular non-PM application, they may ultimately derive considerable joy and professional satisfaction from applying **just enough PM** to help their project teams achieve high-quality results from projects undertaken in their specialties.

Better yet, some of these PM newbies and part timers may ultimately have tremendous impact on the practice of PM in their organizations by gently introducing PM "best practices" that have been "baked in" to the PM tools provided by the PM Profession. For example, while a certified PM professional may be regarded with suspicion by the practitioners of an application specialty, "one of their own" serving in a PM role might be welcomed and get professional-grade results using tools provided by the PM Profession. The result: The organization gently moves forward toward organization-wide PM performance improvement – achieved through a kind of "guerilla" or "grass roots" PM process renewal, instead of formal PM certification and credentialing.

The implications of all this are clear: **Since nearly everyone is (or sometime will be) practicing PM, the PM Profession should create and disseminate solid PM tools and procedures, then provide (or package for distribution) some step-by-step guidance in the use of these** for PM newbies & part timers.

All PM is Local

The definition of the word "project" typically includes the assumption that the outcome will be a "unique product or service..." This uniqueness stems from the special characteristics and goals of the organization undertaking the project and the unique set of circumstances in which the project team operates. In other words, **it is the specific local conditions that determine project deliverables; stakeholders and their relationships; customer/sponsor requirements; regulatory and market forces; best practices of application specialists who are on the team; and many other dimensions of the project.** Even more relevant to any discussion of PM competency is that the local organization determines whether their projects will be managed by full-time, stand-alone project managers or part-time project managers who are also doubling as application specialists/contributors. And, finally, it is the local organization that determines whether those practicing PM must meet particular requirements for formal or informal PM training or some sort of formal PM certification.

The point is this: **As anyone can plainly see, all PM is practiced locally. It is not practiced in some idealized, generic PM world. So why should we expect generic PM certifications to be welcomed or to have wide applicability in bringing about local performance improvement?** Is it any wonder that application specialists who want to increase their PM skills are put off by the many hurdles they must overcome to become "certified?" When they begin to scrutinize the certification requirements, many of these folks see that the certification criteria simply don't ring true, nor do they seem to offer any immediate practical application in helping them solve the unique, local PM problems they face.

So PM Performance Improvement Must Be Managed Locally

It's clear that any attempt at improving an organization's overall PM performance must take into consideration all of the unique local dynamics discussed above. And the best way to assure that these are properly factored in is to manage PM performance improvement initiative locally.

Specifically, such **local PM performance initiatives must accommodate:**

- All **career development initiatives** already in place (or planned) by HR & training people (This includes non-PM-related initiatives.)

- **The organization's overall (including non-PM) curriculum,** training, mentoring, and coaching infrastructure

- All the organization's **competency assessment mechanisms**

- The **strategic goals** of the organization

- **Anything else that could serve as an input or challenge to local PM** performance improvement efforts

How to Bring About Meaningful PM Performance Improvement

So PM is everywhere, it is eventually undertaken by nearly everybody, and the improvement of PM performance must be managed locally. But how?

The diagram below illustrates how meaningful PM performance improvement can be achieved by conquering poor PM performance locally, one organization at a time. As shown, **it is the HR people, the training people, and the individuals seeking to improve their PM**

skills who ought to be driving the PM performance improvement process, not the PM Profession. The former bring to the performance improvement process the "deep knowledge" of the local issues and local PM practices that ultimately make or break the effective performance of project teams. And they have a grasp of the local training, evaluation, and mentoring mechanisms that are needed to monitor and support the development of meaningful PM skills. In short, **they are best positioned to implement the organization's PM renewal.**

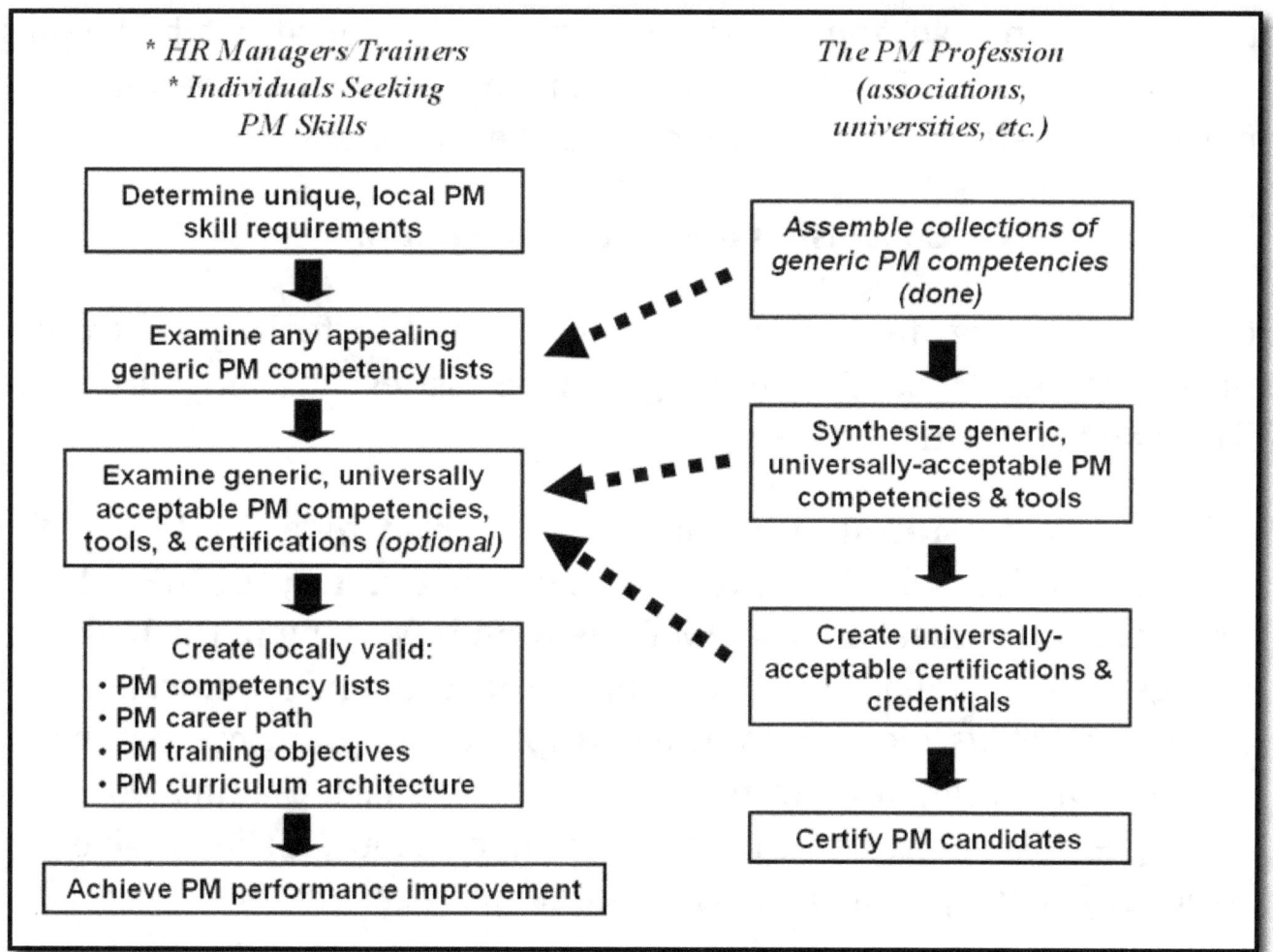

PM Performance Improvement vs. PM Certification

In contrast, the PM Profession (which necessarily exists outside the local contexts of individual organizations) is shown to be properly engaged in the resolution of the broad, generic PM issues. So what might appear to a local HR person to be fairly esoteric debates about the finer points of PM vision and values becomes, appropriately, the responsibility of the PM Profession. In turn, the outputs of the PM Profession's efforts (i.e., the thorny generic issues resolved) are used as illuminating inputs to support substantive, locally-meaningful PM performance improvement. In this way, the efforts of all those in the PM Profession who are now scrambling to describe (or capture for themselves?) the "one true" set of ideal PM skills and practices may have value far above and beyond that of mere certification of a handful of PM elites. Instead, their work can serve all organizations by helping to enhance (dare I say "professionalize?") the PM performance improvement efforts of local organizations everywhere.

Conclusion and Recommendations

Besides exorcising my personal demons related to feeling a "stranger in a strange land," **sorting through these issues has led me to the following recommendations:**

- **The PM Profession should work toward creating a single set of generic, universally-acceptable PM competencies, tools, and certifications.** After all, the PM Profession is working in the realm of the generic, as opposed to the realm of the local and specific. So there is little justification for the multiple, overlapping competency schemes and evaluation frameworks with which Dr. Giammalvo struggled. To strengthen the PM Profession's clout, it should give voice to a single, unified and consistent message.

- **HR and training people, as well as those individuals seeking to upgrade their PM skills should (at least, for the present) ignore the certifications put forth by the PM Profession. They should focus instead on simply using the lists of competencies that underlie those certifications as inputs to their own PM performance improvement processes.** In the end, such locally-inspired PM performance improvement efforts are likely to achieve more meaningful, long-term results.

Related Information and Links

So, you might be asking: "Who is this guy to be making such assertions?" Or you may simply want to investigate some of the topics discussed above a little more thoroughly. Below is **a list of my related publications which provide more information and some modest evidence of my credibility on this topic:**

- **"Beyond Sales Training: Designing a Learning Organization, [PDF file]"** [http://www.michaelgreer.com/beyond-sales-training.pdf] from In Action: Designing Training Programs, American Society for Training and Development (ASTD), 1996 ["18 case studies from the real world of training"] ISBN 1-56286-057-7

This book chapter describes exactly how we executed a comprehensive performance analysis to create job models, career paths, curriculum architecture, and corresponding training priorities. While the chapter documents a sales training intervention, I also used a similar approach to develop a proprietary (confidential) PM-related job model and support system for a major global corporation. Read this if you would like to learn specifically what's involved in the development of job models, career paths, curriculum architectures, and so on.

- **Summary of Key Project Manager Actions and Results**

This document (created in 1996) resulted when I worked with a team of veteran project manager reviewers to tease out 20 key PM competencies out of PMI's initial PMBOK (clearly a body of KNOWLEDGE as opposed to a set of competencies). It was the road map that helped me create my best-selling HRD Press text/tool collection, *The Project Manager's Partner.*

- **The New Project Manager's Support Pyramid: A Framework for PM Training & Support**

A web-published article. (The title says it all.)

- **Typical HPT Project Life Cycles**

An excerpt from "Chapter 6: Planning and Managing Human Performance Technology Projects," *Handbook of Human Performance Technology*, San Francisco, Jossey-Bass, 1999

- **Overview of my 1992 book ID Project Management: Tools & Techniques for Instructional Designers & Developers**

This is the first-ever (and possibly the only) book about how to manage the process of instructional design and development.

- **My Custom Workshops**

I've learned a lot of practical and profound stuff about PM from my clients by designing, redesigning and teaching these sessions. In particular, by prepping these sessions, I've learned a great deal about the difficulties faced by training and HR people as they work to upgrade PM practices. (See also my client list.)

SEVEN BENEFITS OF LOCAL PM CERTIFICATION

Why Pursuing Locally-Relevant PM Skills Makes More Sense Than Buying Generic, External PM Certifications

Building on the previous chapter's assertions that "all PM is local," this expanded discussion in PDF form* explains why it makes more sense for an HR or training department to create a unique, organization-specific PM (project management) certification program instead of adopting an external PM certification such as those sold by PMI, PRINCE2, etc.

In a nutshell, the Seven Benefits presented are:

- Targeted Skills

- Briefer, More Relevant Training

- No "Client Dependency"

- A Practical, Common Sense PM Culture Instead of a PM Elite

- Lower Training and Maintenance Costs

- Less Portable Certifications

- Local HR Control & Integration

To get the entire 6-page article, download this PDF:

* Seven Benefits of Local PM Certification: Why Pursuing Locally-Relevant PM Skills Makes More Sense Than Buying Generic, External

PM Certifications (http://michaelgreer.biz/7-Benefits-of-Local-PM-Certification.pdf)

HOW TO CREATE A LOCALLY-RELEVANT SET OF PM JOB TASKS AND COMPETENCIES BASED ON JOB LEVEL

(Note: The primary audience of this chapter is the person who is responsible for establishing and maintaining an organization's training and development efforts – particularly as these relate to project management (PM). A secondary audience might be someone working with an organization's project management office [PMO] who wants to create a structured PM career path to be monitored and supported by the PMO.)

This chapter summarizes a process by which you can create a comprehensive, locally-relevant set of **"PM Job Tasks and Competencies Based on Job Level"** that can serve as the foundation of your organization's unique PM Job Model. This, in turn, can be used as a powerful reference tool to guide the evolution of each project manager's individual career, including helping structure performance evaluations, coaching, PM training and education, and HR initiatives related to PM and PM career development.

The Steps to Follow

Below, in a highly condensed form, are the steps to follow. (*Note*: Some of these steps — those marked with an * — are discussed in greater detail, with links to helpful resources, in my free 16-page PDF titled *Do-It-Yourself PM Certification: How to Document Your Skills & Get the Credibility You've Earned without Jumping Through Someone Else's Hoops* — http://michaelgreer.biz/?p=1450).

1. Find a comprehensive list of generic PM skills (asapm, GAPPS, Prince2, PMBOK, etc.).*
2. Study your chosen list of skills to be sure you understand the implications of each skill for PM job performance.*
3. Edit this list and use it as the foundation to create your own, unique, comprehensive list of PM skills.*
4. Contact project managers, supervisors, respected colleagues, experts, customers, or anyone who might help you refine and edit this list and ask them to provide detailed input.* (Consider using formal information gathering tools or processes such as those used to support a needs analysis, performance analysis, etc.)
5. Summarize the annotated skills list and sequence them according to a logical progression that would reflect a PM career in your organization.
6. Create a draft PM Job Tasks & Competencies Based on Job Level (See example below.)
7. Share this draft with anyone who participated in Step 4 (above) and ask for their feedback, changes, etc.
8. Revise and finalize your PM Job Tasks & Competencies Based on Job Level and begin integrating it into your a) PM performance evaluations, b) PM coaching, c) PM training and education and d) related HR initiatives.

Sample Table: PM Job Tasks & Competencies Based on Job Level

Below is a "genericized" table showing **PM Job Tasks & Competencies Based on Job Level.** This sample is derived from one I created as part of an extensive PM Requirements Analysis for a large, multi-national client. Several in-depth, formal needs analysis and performance analysis techniques preceded the creation of this document, including in-depth structured interviews with project managers and their supervisors, analysis of existing PM training, creation of hypothesized skills lists and refinement of these by interviewees, etc.

Sample of Typical PM Job Tasks and Competencies Based on Job Level

PM Job Task (Skill)	Not Proficient or Empowered	Proficient, Requires Direction	Proficient, Self-Initiating	Able to coach, advise others
Legend: ▲ Senior Proj. Mgr.; △ Proj. Mgr.; ◆ Project Expeditor/Tracker; ● Technical Lead; ○ Team Member				
1.0 Project Start				
1.1 Support the Project Sales Manager throughout the Proposal with estimates for PM, site management, integration and technical activity, proposal schedule, risk, and any other requested information, as appropriate.	○	●,◆	△	▲
1.2 Prepare and help conduct (if applicable) or attend a Sales Turnover Meeting to receive the information itemized on the Project Transmittal Form.	○	●,◆	△	▲
1.3 Review the contract documents and take corrective action, if required, through a Project Risk Analysis or Overrun Alert and associated mitigation plans.	○	●,◆	△	▲
1.3.1 Authorize project start after receipt of a signed contract or official POE.	○,●,◆		△	▲
1.4 Set up project documentation files to be maintained throughout the life of the project.		○,●,◆	△	▲
1.5 Make active project files accessible at all times.		○,●,◆	△	▲
1.6 Select and perform appropriate tasks related to Initiating a project or project phase.[g]	○	●,◆	△	▲
1.6.1 Demonstrate project need and feasibility.[g]	○	●,◆	△	▲
1.6.2 Obtain authorization for the project as a whole and for each project phase.[g]	○,●,◆		△	▲
2.0 Project Planning				
2.1 Develop the Project Plan.	○	●◆	△	▲
2.1.1 Create a Preliminary Plan/Schedule using the Matrix method, or if required by contract, the CPM method.	○●	◆	△	▲

Sample table: PM tasks/competencies X job level

Click here to view/download the full, 7-page PDF of this table — (http://michaelgreer.biz/Greers-Generic-PM-Job-Tasks-&-Competencies-Based-on-Job-Level.pdf)

The **sample Tasks/Competencies table is based on five levels in the evolution of a project manager within the organization.** These levels, listed in order of increasing PM sophistication, include:

1. Project Team Member
2. Technical Lead
3. Project Expeditor/Tracker
4. Project Manager
5. Senior Project Manager

For each of these evolutionary stages, the table illustrates:

- **The task or skill to be performed** — These are listed in the context of the client's typical project life cycle and some PMBOK competencies which were deemed to be locally important.

- **The skill level to be attained by a particular level of PM performer** — These range from the lowest skill level ("Not Proficient or Empowered") to "Proficient, Requires Direction" to "Proficient, Self-Initiating" to the highest level "Able to coach, advise others."

Some Examples to Illustrate

To see how this table works, examine it as you **consider these examples:**

- **For Job Task 1.1 (Support the Project Sales Manager...)**, the average Project Team Member need not be proficient. However, the Technical Lead and the Project Expeditor should be proficient, though requiring some direction and input. At the same time, the Project Manager should be proficient and self-initiating (i.e., not need direction) at this task. Finally, the Senior Project Manager should be able to coach and advise the rest of the project team on this task.

- **In Job Task 1.3.1 (Authorize project start...)**, the Project Team Member, Technical Lead, and Project Expeditor/Tracker are simply not empowered. In contrast, the Project Manager is proficient and self-initiating, while the Senior Project Manager is able to coach and advise.

Conclusion

In this article I've described **a process by which you can create a locally-relevant and comprehensive set of PM Job Tasks and Competencies Based on Job Level.** This, in turn, can be used as **a**

powerful reference tool in your organization **to guide** the evolution of each project manager's individual career, namely:

- Performance evaluations
- Coaching
- PM training and education
- HR-related initiatives related to PM and PM career development

ADVANCED PROJECT MANAGEMENT TRAINING: FOCUS ON LOCAL COMPLEXITY, NOT PM ESOTERICA.

(Note: The primary audience of this chapter is the person who is responsible for establishing and maintaining an organization's training and development efforts – particularly as these relate to project management (PM). A secondary audience might be someone working with an organization's project management office [PMO] who wants to create a structured PM career path to be monitored and supported by the PMO.)

The choice: cosmic theory or local challenges?

Let's face it: Formal training for experienced project managers is expensive! In addition to the cost of the class and instructor, pulling these seasoned PM veterans away from their jobs can place the projects they are managing at risk. What's more, when you multiply the class hours by the hourly labor rate of that group of high-value "trainees," you are likely to find that your investment is huge! So, **when you decide** to provide an Advanced PM class, you need to make sure you are getting your money's worth! But how do you do that? This chapter provides some perspective.

Well... It's Always About You, Isn't It?

Recently I was asked by a client to present an Advanced Project Management workshop. I had been working with this organization for more than a decade, providing Basic PM training for medical, clinical, IT, and administrative people as part of a comprehensive leadership development program. In these PM Basic classes, we always encourage people to bring real-world project concepts to class so they can apply the PM theory and tools directly to the challenges they face on the job. And, most of the time, people leave these classes with a big ol' stack of flip chart pages and yellow stickies and other notes that they created in class — and which they intend to put to work immediately with their project teams.

So the emphasis in each PM Basics class is always local. It's about applying formal PM techniques, using practical tools, to real-world projects. This way we can be sure they know how to connect their new PM skills to their work. What's more, the feedback from attendees indicated that they appreciated the opportunity to use class time to "get something done" about that project they were facing.

But what about an Advanced Project Management workshop? Would a similarly localized, hands-on training strategy work here? Or would we need to focus on topics that were so complicated they didn't lend themselves easily to the real-world, bring-your-own project approach?

To answer this, we reviewed all sorts of alternatives related to the content and skills needed. Would we focus on the high-level (sometimes esoteric) PM stuff, such as the formal analysis of earned value, risk, critical path, variance, etc. Or would we maintain our emphasis on the local organization and its unique PM challenges and weirdnesses? After considerable debate, we finally made this strategic decision:

"Advanced Project Management means PM that handles the challenges of large or complicated projects within the context of a specific, locally-unique set of organizational complexities."

People who attend our Advanced PM workshop would have to learn how to handle really big or complex projects that jump across all sorts of real organizational boundaries, departmental silos, conflicting missions, etc. So achieving this immediately relevant local focus became our broad training goal. But we needed to drill a little deeper regarding that issue of complexity.

Unique Features of Complex Projects

So, what do we mean by "complex projects?" Here's a summary of what we decided:

- **Deliverables are more complicated.** That is, the deliverables involve:

  - More units (more pieces to be built)

  - Greater variation in units

  - Finished units that must be integrated & synchronized

- **The "people stuff" is more complicated.** Specifically:

  - Stakeholders are drawn from more organizations.

  - The project must satisfy more organizations' needs.

  - The project & team must please more senior managers.

  - The project & team must beg, borrow, and fight harder for resources.

○ The project manager must coordinate people who don't necessarily know each other or share each others' values and missions.

With a clearer picture of our target (i.e., "complex projects"), we were ready to define the broad strategies needed to cope with them more effectively.

Two Broad Strategies for Coping with Complex Projects

In addition to applying all the usual PM strategies and tools that are addressed in our PM Basics class (Charter, WBS, Scope statements, Effort/Duration tables, schedules, etc.), there are two broad strategies that seem particularly important to the success of complex projects:

First, develop a shared vision of "our" project — With so many people involved in complex projects, it's more important than ever to make sure everyone is "singing from the same song book" regarding:

- Work processes (phases, checks & balances, etc.)
- Finished deliverables (look & feel, user expectations, synchronization of results, etc.)

Second, acquire the "management muscle" to get things done across all the boundaries — Any project manager who must jump across organizational boundaries, silos, or departments needs the power to be effective wherever s/he goes! And that means acquiring the management muscle to:

- Take action (quickly, decisively)
- Get & use resources
- Get timely, meaningful approval (closure) of deliverables as they evolve

- Get timely, meaningful senior management engagement in "tie breaking," and other strategic decision-making
- Acquire broad senior management support of the work process

The Training Design

After carefully defining what we meant by "advanced project management" and "complex projects," then defining some broad strategies for coping with complex projects, we were ready to design our home-grown, locally-relevant training experience for our Advanced PM Workshop attendees. In general, the class would be primarily hands-on, case-study driven. There would be very little presentation of concepts, but instead many small assignments that allowed people to engage key Advanced PM issues in the context of local organizational complexity. In developing this highly-customized class, I worked in two domains:

1. **Created a locally-realistic case study that was rich, complex, and could be subdivided among 2 or 3 work groups whose deliverables and work processes had to synchronize.** — Unlike the PM Basics class, where everyone brought their own real-world, stand-alone projects, the Advanced PM students would need to practice dealing with a complex project that would require subdivision, then convergence, of deliverables as well as cross-fertilization of several different teams, and the seeking of approval from many different authorities.

2. **Created a series of more than a dozen step-by-step small group assignments that forced the work teams to create the usual project artifacts (Charter, WBS, etc.) while adding the appropriate complexity.** — After each assignment, the work teams would debrief and compare notes to see that these artifacts (Charter, WBS, etc.) would "hang together" as a large and complex (but cohesive) project. Special emphasis was placed on the selling

and reselling of the project, as well as techniques to achieve the shared vision and management muscle described above.

It's outside the scope of this chapter (and would violate my confidentiality agreement with my client!) to provide much more information about this class. However, if you'd like **to see a complete list of the agenda items**, including the small group assignments, please **click here:** Advanced Project Management: A Fully-Customized, Hands-On Workshop for Your Project Teams (http://michaelgreer.biz/ Greers-Advanced-PM-Brochure-1p.pdf)

Conclusion

When you invest a ton of money and time in training your high-value PM people in your Advanced Project Management class, your training should be immediately relevant, challenging in complexity, and provide lots of opportunity to struggle with, then overcome, real-world (i.e., "advanced") PM obstacles. By focusing your training design on local PM and organizational complexity, instead of the esoterica of formal PM processes, you'll likely get more bang for your buck!

HOW TO FIND MY PUBLICATIONS OR FOLLOW ME

I make most of my informal publications, announcements, etc. at this website (http://worth-sharing.net):

Mike Greer's WORTH SHARING website banner

Here's a **complete list of everything I've ever formally published:**

- Greer's Publications — http://michaelgreer.biz/?page_id=39

My **most popular books** include:

- **The Project Management Minimalist: Just Enough PM to Rock Your Projects! (2nd edition)** —http://michaelgreer.biz/?page_id=636

- **The Project Manager's Partner, 2nd Edition: A Step-by-Step Guide to Project Management** — http://michaelgreer.biz/?p=208

- **ID Project Management: Tools & Techniques for Instructional Designers & Developers** — http://michaelgreer.biz/?p=4253

*(You can learn more about all my books at my **Amazon Author's Page.** — http://www.amazon.com/Michael-Greer/e/B001KIVUFA)*

Here's some info on **my YouTube Channel:**

- *Introduction/Overview of the Channel — https://www.youtube.com/watch?v=lYJMbR9qeGg*

- *General Project Management Videos Playlist:*

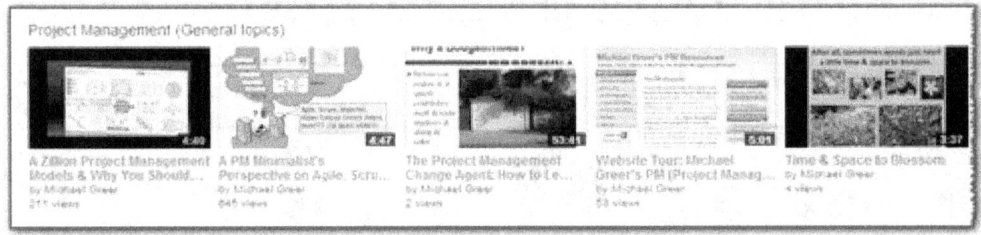

- *Project Management Minimalist Videos Playlist:*

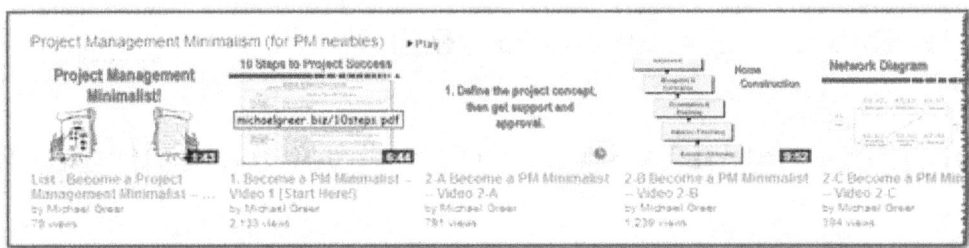

- *The Best Free Training Video Tours Playlist:*

- *Other YouTube Playlists:*

  ◦ Tech Tools & Tips

  ◦ Worth Sharing

  ◦ Project Management Tools & Training for Sale

Finally, I usually announce new publications or videos on one or more of these outlets:

- *My Facebook Page:* https://www.facebook.com/ProjectManagementMinimalist

- *My Twitter feed:* https://twitter.com/michael_greer

- *My Google Plus business page:*
  https://plus.google.com/+MichaelgreerBiz

- *My Google Plus personal page:*
  https://plus.google.com/+MichaelGreer/posts

- *My LinkedIn profile (infrequently updated):*
  https://www.linkedin.com/in/greerspmresources

— Mike G.

ABOUT MY "WORTH SHARING" WEBSITE

Here's the deal. I'm a writer. And as I write this (July, 2015) I've got a bit of a problem: ***My writing keeps popping out of the categories into which I try to squeeze it.*** In the last decade or so, as I've drifted from one new interest to another, I tried to compensate for the shifts by creating new websites to contain the changing topics of my articles, podcasts, and videos.

Trouble is, those nice, tight little buckets labeled *Michael Greer's PM Resources*, *Best Free Training*, *Inspired Project Teams*, and *Project Management Freebies (my four original websites)* finally proved to be too constraining. I continue to learn about — and then try to share with the world — new things that don't always fit neatly into one of these sites. Ultimately this has led to what marketing types might call *"ambiguous brand identity!"*

It is my intent, through my *Worth Sharing* site to address these issues. In particular, I'm attempting to:

1. **Provide a site with enough categories to allow my present and future writing interests to peacefully coexist in one place.** And this means I must not only provide a place for the material that fits into my original buckets (i.e., the four websites named above), but also provide a place to collect entirely new material in some entirely new, and intentionally broad, categories. (Thus you'll find collections vaguely labeled *Editorials, Peace of Mind, Tech, & Misc.!*)

2. **Provide an opportunity for those who choose to uncover my "brand identity" to do so fairly easily by helping them quickly locate everything I've published.** While this won't necessarily make my brand any less ambiguous, it will at least allow readers to more easily form a more complete picture of what I have to offer them.

What My Oldest Colleagues Know

To the casual observer of that intellectual audit trail that is my published works, it may seem I'm somewhat unfocused! However, as my oldest colleagues — the folks who "knew me when" — can tell you, the evolution of my interests has roughly corresponded to the evolution of my career. Specifically, in a professional life that's now exceeded three decades (Whoa!), I've played these roles:

- High school English teacher and university faculty member

- Director of a university Learning Resources (& media production) Center

- Instructional designer/consultant in "performance-based training" for both public & private sector organizations

- Manager of instructional design teams

- Author of PM (project management) books and articles about (at first) managing instructional design and (later) managing any kind of project

- Creator/presenter of customized, on-site PM workshops for many different organizations in many different industries (and several different countries!)

- Student of (and writer about) ways to inspire, motivate, enlighten, and find personal peace of mind as part of a project team and, more importantly, as an individual

- (Throughout it all) a somewhat geeky adopter and explorer of new technologies in the form of media, computer hardware & software, etc.

So given the eclectic list above, my oldest colleagues cut me some slack and tolerate me as I go on and on about the latest thing I've learned in one of these seemingly disconnected domains. They know that while I can sometimes be obnoxious and over-enthusiastic, I generally mean well and have been known to leave my readers with something useful or at least moderately enlightening. And I hope you will come to agree with them.

— Mike Greer
— email: pm.minimalist[at]gmail[dot]com